THE RISE OF
SARASOTA

THE RISE OF
SARASOTA

KEN THOMPSON AND THE REBIRTH OF PARADISE

JEFF LaHURD

Published by The History Press
Charleston, SC 29403
www.historypress.net

Copyright © 2012 by Jeff LaHurd
All rights reserved

Front cover, bottom: Courtesy of Ed Lederman.
All other cover images are courtesy of Barbara Thompson and the Sarasota County History Center.

First published 2012

Manufactured in the United States

ISBN 978.1.60949.834.4

Library of Congress CIP data applied for.

Notice: The information in this book is true and complete to the best of our knowledge. It is offered without guarantee on the part of the author or The History Press. The author and The History Press disclaim all liability in connection with the use of this book.

All rights reserved. No part of this book may be reproduced or transmitted in any form whatsoever without prior written permission from the publisher except in the case of brief quotations embodied in critical articles and reviews.

This book is dedicated with love to my beautiful wife, Jennifer—my Dolly Girl.

CONTENTS

Acknowledgements 9
Introduction 11

1. Welcome to Sarasota 13
2. Thompson Family Travels and Travails 17
3. Rebirth: 1950–1959 29
4. Sarasota Goes Modern and Outward: The 1960s 75
5. Regrouping: The 1970s 97
6. "I Do" 115
7. Trying to Hold On: The 1980s 125
8. Not Quite Time to Say Goodbye 135
9. Goodbye 143
10. Tributes 145

Appendix. A List of Changes During Thompson's Tenure 147
Bibliography 149
Index 153
About the Author 157

ACKNOWLEDGEMENTS

I would like to thank Barbara Thompson for allowing me free access to Ken Thompson's papers and for providing me with many of the photographs I have used in this book. I'm grateful to his children (Ken, Charles and Laura Thompson DeUnger) and his grandchildren (Amanda DeUnger Lewis and Alexandra DeUnger) for corresponding with me. Their memories helped me understand Thompson the family man.

Thank you to my friend Scott Proffitt for helping to edit and make corrections to this book before it went to the publisher.

Thank you to the former mayors and commissioners—Elmer Berkel, Jack Gurney, Kerry Kirschner, Lou Ann Palmer, Rita Roehr and Fred Soto—who helped me understand what it was like to work with Sarasota's long-lived city manager.

Thanks to Ed James, former journalist, community activist and host of the television show *Black Almanac* for his insights into how Thompson integrated the Sarasota Library with a phone call. And also to Bruce E. Franklin, president of Land Resource Strategies, LLC, and Paul Thorpe, "Mister Downtown Sarasota," for sharing their knowledge of how Thompson "got things done."

Most of the photographs in this book that were not supplied by Mrs. Thompson were from the collection at the Sarasota County History Center, and most of those came from the George I. "Pete" Esthus Collection.

INTRODUCTION

Twenty-five years have come and gone since Ken Thompson was forced to leave the city manager position he came to define. And just as the Sarasota he arrived in to take up his duties on February 1, 1950, was shaped by the land boom of the 1920s, so too has today's Sarasota been shaped by his thirty-eight-year tenure as the longest-serving city manager in the nation.

Early on, he had a vision of what Sarasota could become, and slowly, methodically and with a cautious eye on the city coffers, he helped mold this beautiful city to that vision.

During his time in office, nearly three dozen mayors came and went, as did countless city commissioners and myriad city personnel. He was the constant, the captain at the helm of a ship with an ever-changing crew. He was the consummate professional; his intelligence, honesty and integrity were unquestioned. Elmer Berkel, one of the mayors Thompson served in the 1970s, called him the most brilliant man he had ever met. Another mayor, Jack Gurney, thought of him as a patrician gentleman.

Thompson brought to the job an analytical mind and a penurious nature with the tax dollar that would prevent a throw-money-at-it approach to problem solving. He had a deep-seated belief in the commissioner/city manager form of local government, and when he came to Sarasota from Miami Beach, he said he had come to stay, and stay he did.

He was thirty-nine years old when he was hired, seventy-seven when he retired and ninety-one when he passed away, remembered, as *Sarasota Herald-*

Introduction

Tribune editor Waldo Proffitt put it, "for his rock-solid integrity in private and public life. It is at the core of his legacy and it is the quality by which he would most want to be measured."

Proffitt called him the "architect of Sarasota."

1

WELCOME TO SARASOTA

He doesn't manipulate the commissioners, but sometimes he'll drag his feet a little until he thinks it's right.
—*Mayor William Overton*

In 1950, the city of Sarasota was very much as it had been since the first major development spurt of the frenetic 1920s. In fact, if you came to town in 1925 and returned in 1950, except for the addition of some major Works Progress Administration projects in the 1930s, you would have seen very little change.

The predominant architecture was still the Mediterranean Revival, Spanish Mission or Neoclassical of old. Roads were narrow, two lanes, and deteriorating. Traffic lights were scant. City business was conducted in the old Hover Arcade building at the foot of lower Main Street on the bay and would be into the 1960s. The pace was relaxed, the out islands practically devoid of development.

Downtown in the early 1950s was still the center of Sarasota's universe, filled with lounges, hotels, restaurants, two theaters, churches, car dealers, department stores, drugstores and banks (there were just three), and as U.S. Highway 41 still ran along Main Street, gas stations lined the way to service the stream of cars and trucks passing through town.

There were only four tall buildings within the city limits, all built in the mid-1920s: the Sarasota Terrace Hotel, the Orange Blossom Hotel, the Hotel Sarasota and the Palmer Bank.

The Rise of Sarasota

The bridge to Lido, built by John Ringling and gifted to the city in 1927, was showing its age in the 1950s, while the Siesta Bridge was frightfully narrow and the Stickney Point Bridge was still a one-lane, hand-cranked swivel bridge.

The local roads of 1950 needed repair and widening, the water/sewer system was in urgent need of upgrade and the mosquito problem, especially during the evening hours of summer, was desperate.

Most visitors still arrived here by car, train or bus, and the Sarasota-Bradenton Airport was better suited to a small town rather than a city striving to capture its share of the post–World War II boom and move forward.

During the off-season, business revenue fell so dramatically that store owners sometimes closed their stores at noon to go fishing, hopeful that they had made enough revenue during the snowbird season to tide them through the lean summer months.

And while many recall these laid-back days with nostalgic fondness, they forget that from its earliest years Sarasota was not about being relaxed and slow paced but rather about growth, about selling real estate and attracting tourists and newcomers and about the requisite development to invite and accommodate them.

With the notable exception of Bertha Palmer, Sarasota's early leaders were mostly real estate people and developers: John Hamilton Gillespie, Harry Higel, A.B. Edwards, Joseph Lord, Owen Burns, John and Charles Ringling and countless others. They were visionary capitalists, aware of Sarasota's potential, who strove to fulfill the town's early motto: "May Sarasota Prosper," adopted in 1902.

The board of trade, which morphed into the chamber of commerce, was also a strong, pro-growth voice, as were Sarasota's newspapers: the *Sarasota Times*, the *Sarasota Herald*, *This Week in Sarasota*, the *Daily Tribune* and *The News*. So, too, were the local service clubs, particularly the Woman's Club, the Kiwanis Club and the Rotary Club.

Miscues abounded during the freewheeling '20s. Longtime realtor Roger Flory recalled the "fortune hunters" who came to Sarasota from all over the country to speculate in real estate and development. "They gave no thought to drainage, utilities or other improvements."

The city's first mayor, A.B. Edwards, reflected:

> *It was worse than the mad rush to the ancient gold fields. The town filled up overnight with land speculators and subdivision boys...Street corners were used for offices. Contracts and option blanks were carried in pockets.*

Welcome to Sarasota

They were sleeping in cars, on street benches, and actually in the railroad waiting rooms... The high-pressure boys were walking around with checks in their pockets for several days, too busy to deposit them in banks. Then, about the latter part of 1926, the high-pressure boys were trading among themselves, wondering what happened; and by early 1927, the big real estate boom was all over. The water had been squeezed out of the sponge.

Those leading Sarasota in the 1940s did not want another freewheeling, speculative real estate bubble that, upon bursting, would leave the taxpayers footing the costs for services and infrastructure improvements from taxes that could not be collected.

They correctly deduced that after the war, Sarasota would once again become a go-to destination for tourists and newcomers wishing to start their lives anew here—young couples wanting to raise families and retirees wishing to settle here for their remaining years.

As World War II was coming to an end, community leaders felt that a true professional would be required to guide the city through the next growth spurt and opted to institute a new system of local government.

Sentiment for the change was strong. At the end of 1944, the City Government Committee of the Sarasota County Chamber of Commerce polled its members and found that 350 agreed to the change, while only 7 wanted to keep the status quo. At the polls, the citizens echoed the sentiment for change by voting for it 1,499 to 405 against.

In those days, pride in a job well done was the only pay sought by Sarasota's elected officials. In an article in the *Evening Gazette* by John W. Bloomer, the commissioner/manager seemed an idyllic system of government. He spelled out exactly how it worked:

Under the charter, all commissioners are elected on an at-large basis. There are no wards, no precincts, or precinct political organizations. There are no political debts to pay after the election. Commissioners are barred by the charter from even recommending personnel hirings and firings to the city manager. Agreement to become a candidate for the commission is considered a civic contribution, and with the expectation that the only remuneration for the commissioner will be the gratitude of the community.

The new city charter was approved in a special election on November 5, 1945, and on February 1, 1946, Colonel Ross E. Windom was hired at $9,000 per year for the new position. According to his son, Dr. Robert

Windom, he had been offered $13,000 to start but turned that salary down because, after looking at the city's books, he determined the commissioners could not afford that amount.

Approached again, he took the $9,000; the city had enough in its coffers for that amount.

Windom had been the city manager of Westerville and Portsmouth, Ohio. He promised a flexible government that could respond quickly to the needs of the people. According to the *Tampa Tribune*, his three-point program called for the appointment of a planning board and rezoning of the city, adoption of a pay-as-you-go plan of city government and equalization of property assessments.

Having served in World War I, Colonel Windom ran a tight ship, with city hall being known as Fort Windom. He paid special attention to the needs of Sarasota Bay, and it was his idea to form an auxiliary for Sarasota's municipal hospital. He stayed in Sarasota for two years before moving on to accept the city manager job in St. Petersburg.

Carl H. Bischoff from Washington, D.C., took over on July 1, 1948, but served only briefly. Conflicting with the city commissioners, he did not make it through his second six-month probationary period. He said his ouster came as a complete surprise.

Enter Ken Thompson.

2

THOMPSON FAMILY TRAVELS AND TRAVAILS

Rich experiences in an island paradise.
—*Ken Thompson*

Four months after Bertha Palmer fell in love with Sarasota and proclaimed Sarasota Bay more beautiful than the bay of Naples, and a month after Owen Burns bought what today would be 75 percent of the city limits of Sarasota, Kenneth Thompson was born on La Isla De Pinos, the Isle of Pines, in the West Indies, fifty miles off the coast of Cuba, on June 23, 1910.

He was the seventh and last child of Kathleen and Charles Thompson, she Irish, he a Scot who worked from 1889 until 1904 at the Great Northern Railway of London before leaving England to pursue, but never attain, good fortune in the New World.

They and two surviving children, George and Doris, left for Canada in the early 1900s. Staying only briefly, they bore another child, Yvonne, and moved on to New Jersey, where a son, Roy, was born.

Financial success continued to elude them, and in 1908 the wanderers learned of a small, beautiful and undeveloped island off Cuba called the Isle of Pines, which had become an American territory after the Spanish-American War. With its rich soil and tropical weather, it beckoned adventurous souls wishing to take a gamble: an opportunity at farming.

Here, the Thompsons would reside in the small community of Santa Barbara, on the northwest section of the island, where Charles would try his luck growing grapefruit on a ten-acre tract, while Kathleen would

THE RISE OF SARASOTA

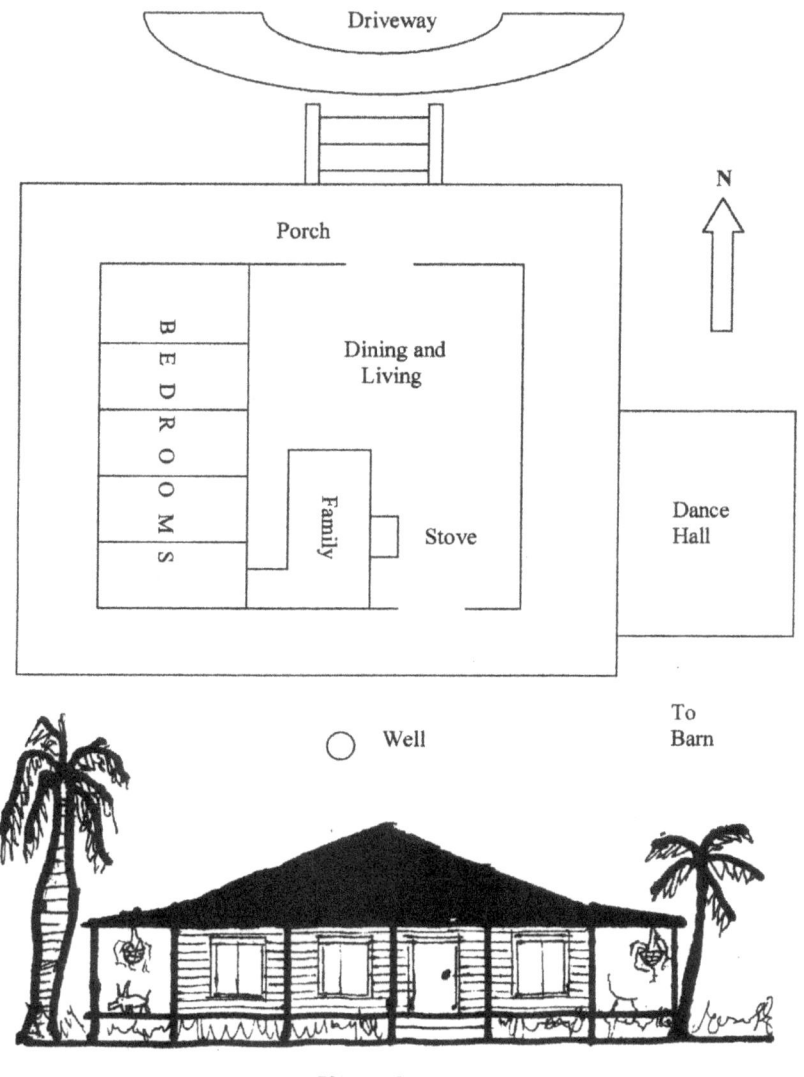

Ken Thompson's drawing of his mother's Norwood Inn on Isle of Pines, where he was born. It was situated on ten acres of property that his father was farming. *Courtesy Barbara Thompson.*

run a small inn and dance hall in what Ken Thompson remembered as a "primitive frame farmhouse" on the property.

Although the island was beautiful, rife with tall pine trees, royal palm trees and colorful tropical foliage and surrounded by azure water and bright, white sandy beaches, life there must have been difficult. Santa Barbara offered few amenities. Among its few wood-frame buildings were a grocery and hardware store, and there was a field used for baseball.

They christened their establishment Norwood Inn, after the north woods of England of which Mrs. Thompson had been so fond. A drawing of the inn, situated among palm trees, mango trees and the grapefruit grove, reveals an open wraparound porch, five bedrooms for guests, a family section for the Thompson clan and a communal dining and living area with a wood-burning stove. The small dance hall was attached to the east side of the inn, and candles, kerosene lamps and one carbide fixture provided light.

The inn was made of Caribbean pine with no windows and only shutters to keep the weather out. Without screens, mosquitoes were a significant problem, particularly during the rainy season. Everyone slept under mosquito nets.

The Norwood Inn, with its tiny dance hall, lacked indoor plumbing and had no electricity and one outhouse. A horse-drawn wagon was used for transportation to the nearby town, a well in the backyard provided water and a barn on the property completed the picture.

Farming, of course, especially in pre-mechanized days, was a labor-intensive, seven-day-a-week, morning-till-dawn struggle, working the soil and battling insects and the elements—no easy task, especially during hurricane season, which could wipe away a crop.

Charles chose to farm grapefruit, and other farmers on the Isle of Pines chose guava, mango, watermelon, cocoa, plums, peppers and eggplant for export to markets in Canada, Europe and America. There was an abundance of hardwoods on the isle to fashion into novelties for sale abroad.

The lumber business on the island thrived. It was estimated that nearly 10 million feet of lumber were produced there annually.

For seven years, the ambitious family, all participating in the enterprise in one way or another, toiled. The children were schooled at home.

Ken Thompson's recollections include handmade clothes, ordering necessities from the Montgomery-Ward catalogue, playing with his siblings, adventurous sightseeing ventures and a loving, caring and supportive family—a poor but happy childhood in what was a combination of a lovely paradise/harsh wilderness. Not too unlike Sarasota during those same years.

Thompson vividly remembered the hurricane of 1916, a weeklong storm that battered the inn, damaged the grove and seemed like it would never let up.

For an adventurous youth, there were marble mountains to climb, with caves cut into them to explore and rivers to canoe. Some believed this was the site of Robert Louis Stevenson's *Treasure Island*, and no doubt buried treasure from pirate days was looked for on the island. The island newspaper, *Isle of Pines Appeal*, conjectured that as a rendezvous of pirates like Morgan, there were probably stores of gold and silver buried or hidden in the caves.

His sister Doris, whom Thompson remembered "as wonderful as anyone could get among the five billion or so people on this planet," married islander Ernest Gruppe and moved to nearby Santa Fe. There they operated many enterprises, including a movie house, a saloon, a radio/phonograph repair shop, a grocery store and a bakery. Santa Fe also boasted a mineral springs, which flowed into a creek; a smattering of homes; and an American school.

Due to the changing political landscape affecting the status of the island, the Thompsons and other families who were drawn to it begrudgingly left, feeling betrayed by the American government, which encouraged their migration.

Thompson indicated that the island was ceded to Cuba in exchange for Guantanamo Naval Base, which would ultimately affect trade by adding U.S. tariffs to fruits and vegetables sent to the States, cutting an already slim profit margin and decreasing property values no longer under the protection of the American flag.

Once again, the Thompsons, with three of their children—Kenneth, seven; Roy, eight; and Yvonne, ten—were on the move.

They were picked up by Ernest and Doris and taken to Santa Fe, where they stayed the night. Then it was a drive to Jucaro to board the steamship SS *Cristobal Colon* for the overnight journey to Batabano, Cuba, and then, by train, to Havana.

In 1917, a car ride, ship voyage and train trip was impressive to a boy of seven and remembered fondly.

Of the decision to leave, Thompson wrote:

Thompson Family Travels and Travails

Although the rich experiences of a youngster growing in a tropical island environment in a family that cared, if continued, probably did not offer as much opportunity for a fulfilling future as I was later to experience as an engineer and City Manager, and other rewarding life experiences, like education and family.

The family lived temporarily in a small house on the outskirts of Havana, where Charles got a job with the local railroad. When one of the rail company homes near the Christina Street Station became available, they took up residence there.

With failed stints in Canada and New Jersey and the begrudging move from the Isle of Pines, Charles Thompson, now in a low-paying job in Havana, felt like a failure and became withdrawn. Probably to self-medicate, he began to drink to excess, and Mrs. Thompson became the leader of the family. Thompson wrote that his father's drinking had a major effect on his lifetime abhorrence of alcohol.

An opportunity for Mrs. Thompson to operate a sugar mill called Central Socorro in central Cuba became available, and she took it. This, too, failed, and the five Thompsons were off to Cayo Maso, a mining, cement-manufacturing and shipping port north of Mariel, Cuba.

Here the family lived in a company house, "in a very nice environment of mostly American managers and workers." Charles worked in the cement plant.

The fortunes of the family must have taken a decided, if temporary, turn for the better, as Thompson recalled that Yvonne got a pony for her birthday.

But after only a year, for reasons not known to Thompson, the family was off again, this time to a sugar mill run by the Hershey Corporation, which produced sugar for its chocolate. Here, too, living conditions were good, "but there was no promise of an adequate future."

While many Americans living on the Isle of Cuba sent their children to America for their education, the Thompsons could not afford this luxury and decided it was time to leave Cuba for Florida.

Thompson reasoned, "This was done for the purpose of educating the kids and for the deeper reason that all of the previous endeavors were failures and if this trend was to continue, it might as well be in an English speaking country."

In 1922, aboard the steamship *Cuba*, the family set sail from Havana to Key West and then across Henry Flagler's Overseas Railroad to mainland Florida, "leaving behind a trail of frustrated attempts to find a place in the scheme of things for a British family in the new world."

The Rise of Sarasota

In Florida, the family lived in Miami, Fort Lauderdale, Miami Beach and Palm Beach, where Charles worked on the estate of Mr. and Mrs. E.T. Stotesbury, called El Mirasol, which had been designed by Addison Mizner. Kathleen ran a small boardinghouse.

Thompson's first son, Charles, said his grandfather found stability there, gaining a reputation as a bird and plant collector. His expertise on how to care for tropical bird species allowed him to publish an article in *Aviculture* magazine about the difficult process of hand breeding macaws.

Not long after the family's return to the States, Thompson, not quite a teenager but with a spirit of adventure welling up in him, longed for the Isle of Pines. He set off on his own to Key West but could not find a ship willing to take a twelve-year-old traveling alone back to Cuba, and he returned home.

The two older brothers had set off for sea, with George Thompson becoming a commander in the United States Coast Guard, and Roy, sailing out of San Francisco, California, a chief engineer.

Ken attended Ida M. Fisher High School in Miami Beach, where he was a bright student and a standout athlete. He served as president of the Athletic Council and was president of the Student Council. He was named co-captain and catcher for the *Miami Herald*'s all-star baseball team, hitting over .440 one year, and was a highly rated basketball player. He also lettered in football and swimming.

Taking a lead from his seafaring brothers, after high school he took a job aboard a tanker, trying to earn money for college. He ended up in New Orleans, stayed there only briefly, then bought a motorcycle and drove back to Miami.

He entered the University of Florida, majoring in electrical engineering, and was a good student. To maintain his high academic achievement, he cut out all the sports he had participated in high school save baseball.

At the University of Florida, he was a standout in the outfield and then at first base, known as a dependable player and also for his "splendid hitting." He was called "Slim" and lettered in baseball three years, with a batting average of .300. He graduated in 1936.

During the summer months, he played semipro baseball, traveling around the state, but declined an offer to continue and began his professional career with the city of West Palm Beach as a draftsman.

A young Ken Thompson sailing at Cedar Key, 1938. Sailing was a lifelong passion. Among his last boats was a thirty-eight-foot sloop, which he could sail alone. He said it was the best exercise ever. *Courtesy Barbara Thompson.*

Thompson was a standout baseball player for the University of Florida. He was the Gator lead-off man in 1935, and his position was shifted from the outfield to first base. In those days, they called him "Slim." He went on to play semipro ball, traveling throughout the state. *Courtesy Barbara Thompson.*

Second Lieutenant Kenneth Thompson at work in the South Pacific during World War II. He served in the Army Air Corps, Signal Corps, and was discharged after the war as a captain. *Courtesy Barbara Thompson.*

He courted and married Virginia Leigh Acker, built a modest bungalow and continued to pursue his life-long passion for sailing in the couple's scow-shaped dingy, *Pancake*.

Thompson soon took his drafting skills to Miami Beach and worked his way into the Engineering Department, where he stayed until World War II broke out and he was given a direct commission as a second lieutenant.

According to Charles, while in the service he was selected to work with Watson Watt on Cent metric radar, cavity magnetrons and wave guides at the Massachusetts Institute of Technology.

Thompson served in the Pacific, in the Army Air Force, Signal Corps, as an airborne electronics maintenance officer.

Charles recalled that his father had some responsibility for the installation of airborne bomb site radar in B-24 Liberators.

He was honorably discharged a captain in 1946, sailing back home aboard an 11,450-ton troop transport ship, the USS *General Weigel*, stuffed with nearly 5,000 other servicemen all anxious to get back to the States.

Thompson in uniform, 1943. When he was mustered out of the service in 1946, he sailed home from Manila with thousands of other returning servicemen; quarters were tight and the trip long, and he plotted the course on a homemade sextant. *Courtesy Barbara Thompson.*

He described the two-stack ship the *General Weigel* as a beauty. "Sleek as a race horse." It could cruise at twenty-two knots.

The ship left from Manila Harbor, and to track its progress and plot the course, Thompson devised a rudimentary sextant from bits of Plexiglas and aluminum and took daily readings, which he shared with his fellow officers. He pinned the movement of the ship on a *National Geographic* map he always carried with him when he traveled. He kept the sextant for the remainder of his life.

He used the GI Bill to learn to fly, which became a passion, learning in a J3 floatplane. He later purchased a seventy-five-horsepower Ercoupe, which he kept briefly.

After the senior Charles Thompson was finally able to retire, he and Kathleen decided to take a trip to Hawaii, but before they sailed from California, Charles passed away.

Kathleen returned to Palm Beach, where she died at age eighty-seven.

3
REBIRTH

1950-1959

When I go to Sarasota, I'm going with the intention of staying.
—Ken Thompson

The buzz words of the day for the nation and Sarasota were "progress" and "modern." The country was entering the second half of the twentieth century, and the *Sarasota Herald-Tribune* began the New Year with a twelve-page insert titled "Fifty Years of Progress," with a cover photo of Sarasota's Main Street in 1900 placed above the same scene taken in 1950. The contrast was striking.

Articles focused on the great national strides made in travel, science, medicine and the media and social changes from the Gibson Girl to the controversial Kinsey Report. America came out of World War II number one in the world and proud of it.

Sarasota was poised to move forward, and Sarasota mayor John Fite Robertson, an attorney, was certain that in Kenneth Thompson, the assistant city manager of Miami Beach, the commission had found the perfect person to help guide the city toward the twenty-first century. The commission voted unanimously to offer him the job at $9,000 per year. Later, Robertson said how proud he was the day that he and Thompson closed the deal over a telephone call.

Mayor Robertson and the other commissioners had been tipped off about Thompson by George F. Higgins, a well-known Sarasota water and sewer contractor who had done work in Miami Beach and was familiar with Thompson and his reputation as a good man who could get things done.

The popular and long-serving mayor E.A. Smith, center, standing in front of the city's new sanitation trucks, 1945. Water, sewer and sanitation issues were high on Thompson's to-do list when he first arrived in Sarasota. *Sarasota County History Center.*

Former city commissioner Ben Drymon, reflecting on Thompson's hiring, said:

> *We had trouble with our city manager* [Bischoff] *and had to discharge him. We had heard of Ken Thompson from Miami Beach and we went down to interview him. We invited him up to the city to meet the entire commission, and he was unanimously elected to be our city manager.*

In those days, city managers were usually drawn from the ranks of engineers as they were well versed with the infrastructure issues with which growing Florida towns were wrestling.

When Thompson resigned his position at Miami Beach, one of the most popular resorts in the country, that municipality extended his leave for five months, gave him a month's vacation with pay, lauded his ability and sterling record and hoped he would return. He promised he would not.

Thompson had been acting city manager during city manager Claude Renshaw's illness, and Mayor Harold Turn said of Thompson's departure,

Rebirth

Thompson and his first wife, Virginia, showing off a wristwatch given to him by the City of Miami Beach in gratitude for his work there. When he left Miami Beach for Sarasota, he announced he was coming to Sarasota to stay, and stay he did. *Courtesy Barbara Thompson.*

"This city is losing one of its finest officials. Sarasota is indeed fortunate to obtain a man of such high caliber."

Although Renshaw had been a mentor to Thompson, a Miami newspaper quipped that Thompson was leaving because "Thompson is too conscientious and high principled to accept the 'open town' policy existing [in Miami Beach]."

Thompson and Virginia put their nearly completed home up for sale; accepted the plaudits of his associates, a gold wristwatch from the thankful city and a gold embossed leather briefcase from his Kiwanis Club; and came to Sarasota with their son Charles.

Thompson avowed, "When I go to Sarasota, I'm going with the full intention of staying."

His membership in the Kiwanis Club was fortunate. Nearly all the men who guided Sarasota's growth and played such an important role in its history were longtime members, among them Owen Burns, Sarasota's first major developer; John Hamilton Gillespie, the Scot who was sent over to revive the efforts of the Florida Mortgage and Investment Company to colonize Sarasota; A.B. Edwards, the first mayor of the city; civic leader Ralph Caples; J.H. Lord, a state legislator who owned vast acreage in the area; and every mayor up to and including Mayor Robertson, as well as Commissioner Ben Drymon and Thompson's predecessor, Ross Windom.

Into the 1970s, many of the city's key players, civic leaders, city officials and downtown businessmen and professionals were Kiwanians of long standing—a close fraternity of men with the same vision of Sarasota that engendered a sense of trust and cooperation.

Initially, some in the community felt the position should have been filled by a local, specifically Charles H. Pickett, the respected city treasurer and tax collector who had been acting city manager since Bischoff was ousted. But the majority felt that Sarasota's most pressing needs, especially the

Opposite, top: A parade on North Pineapple, near Morrison's Cafeteria. Today, this is the site of Robert and Roberta Turoff's Golden Apple Dinner Theatre, which opened on December 18, 1971, with the play *Stop the World, I Want to Get Off*. Thompson loved to take the family to the restaurant for dinner, and after the Golden Apple moved in, he was there every Friday at noon to attend the weekly Kiwanis luncheon meetings. *Sarasota County History Center, Bill Blackstone Collection.*

Opposite, bottom: Big news for Sarasota: the *Sarasota Herald-Tribune* banner headline announces Thompson's appointment as the city's third city manager. *Courtesy Barbara Thompson.*

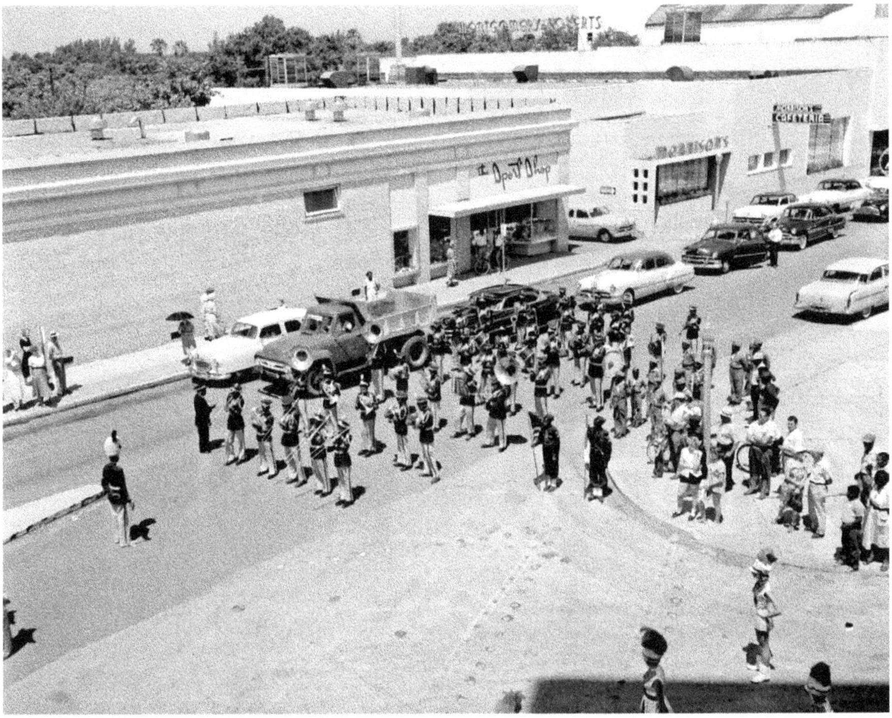

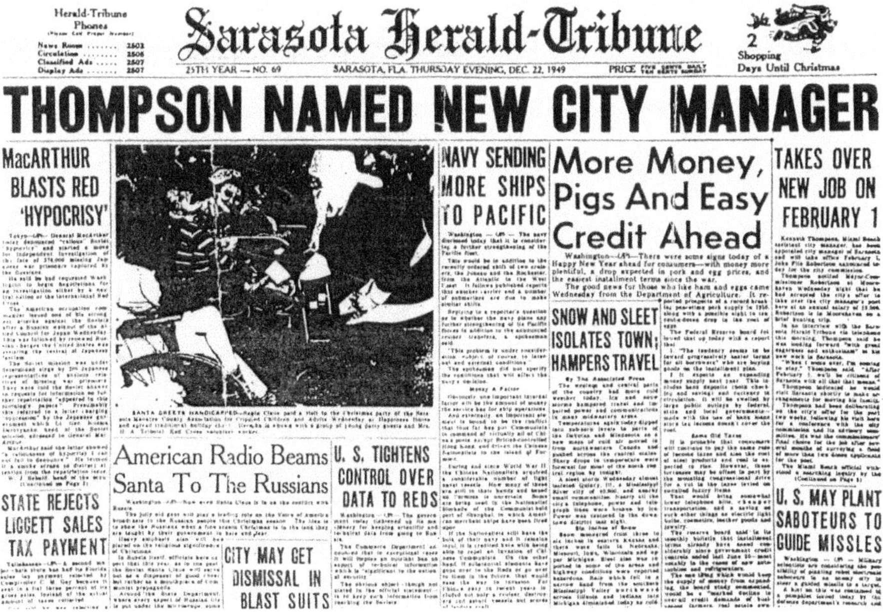

Herald-Tribune Phones

News Room 2503
Circulation 2506
Classified Ads 2507
Display Ads 2507

Sarasota Herald-Tribune

25TH YEAR — NO. 69 SARASOTA, FLA. THURSDAY EVENING, DEC. 22, 1949 PRICE

2 Shopping Days Until Christmas

THOMPSON NAMED NEW CITY MANAGER

MacARTHUR BLASTS RED 'HYPOCRISY'

SANTA GREETS HANDICAPPED

NAVY SENDING MORE SHIPS TO PACIFIC

More Money, Pigs And Easy Credit Ahead

Washington—(AP)—There were some signs today of a Happy New Year ahead for consumers—with money more plentiful, a drop expected in pork and egg prices, and the easiest installment terms since the war.

The good news for those who like ham and eggs came Wednesday from the Department of Agriculture. It re-

SNOW AND SLEET ISOLATES TOWN; HAMPERS TRAVEL

By The Associated Press

TAKES OVER NEW JOB ON FEBRUARY 1

American Radio Beams Santa To The Russians

U. S. TIGHTENS CONTROL OVER DATA TO REDS

STATE REJECTS LIGGETT SALES TAX PAYMENT

CITY MAY GET DISMISSAL IN BLAST SUITS

U. S. MAY PLANT SABOTEURS TO GUIDE MISSLES

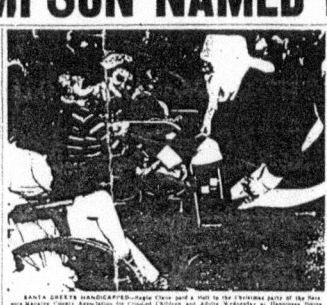

The Rise of Sarasota

When Thompson arrived in Sarasota in 1950, Smacks, the quintessentially popular drive-in restaurant, served the finest hamburgers in town and was a popular place for the younger set to cruise, as in the movie *American Graffiti*. It also offered a full-service menu and was popular with families and downtown businessmen. *Sarasota County History Center, Bill Blackstone Collection.*

sewer/water project and street improvements, required a person with an engineering background. It was also believed that an outsider would not be subjected to the political pressure that a local might encounter.

Thompson drove to Sarasota on January 8, 1950, for a look-see; he met with Pickett and inspected several departments. A photograph on the front page of the *Herald* showed the two men peering at what was depicted as a map of Sarasota's future.

Indeed, with Thompson's arrival, that future was at hand. By the time he retired, the city had changed every bit as much as it had during the preceding "Fifty Years of Progress."

Rebirth

On the face of it, the city commission/city manager form of government is simple. The people elect the commissioners. The commissioners set the policies and hire the manager, who advises them and carries out their policies. Thompson was a true believer in this system, calling it the greatest contribution to American local government.

He officially began his duties on February 1, 1950, working for a city commission that consisted of Mayor/Commissioner John Fite Robertson and Commissioners Jerry Ludwig, Ben J. Drymon, Leroy T. Fenne and W. Mac Harmon.

It's February 1, 1950, and Ken Thompson is taking the oath of office, administered by Mayor John Fite Robertson as other city commissioners and city officials look on. *Courtesy Barbara Thompson.*

At the end of the year, Drymon and Harmon would be replaced by Ralph P. Farrell, a real estate developer, and A.W. Knapp, an oil distributor. According to Karl A. Bickel, longtime Sarasota civic leader and former head of United Press, this commission was the "best brained city council we have had in years; a much better trained city hall outfit due to acting City Manager Charlie Pickett's work over the last seven months."

Thompson refused a contract, indicating that he wanted the commission to feel free to fire him if he did not perform to its expectations and also wishing to be able to leave if and when he so desired.

He and Virginia and Charles moved into a comfortable home on Brywill Circle, and soon he would build a new home in Harbor Acres.

Announcing that he would rely on Pickett until he became familiar with his new post, Thompson was a quick study. His engineer's analytical mind and a philosophy of fiscal conservatism would preclude the missteps of the previous era.

Confident and unexcitable, he was an intellectual admirably equipped for the job. Along with his BA degree, he had obtained a civil engineer's license in design and construction and was a licensed land surveyor. His education was bolstered with postgraduate work at Harvard University and the Massachusetts Institute of Technology.

He never solved problems by throwing money at them. When the city commission sought his guidance, it knew he would study the matter at hand objectively, analyze the issues involved and try to get as much accomplished as he could for the city taxpayers with the least possible taxes. Throughout his long tenure, this was his modus operandi.

He was a firm believer of planning, which he said was sometimes a hard sell to those who wanted to move quickly. "Planning," he said, "is a way of doing things economically. An investment in proper planning will bring handsome returns."

That philosophy guided him throughout his career.

And through the post–World War II rush of new housing developments, he called for a "high standard of subdivision control…so that the subdivision could better be able to pay its own way."

Early on in his administration, he said that one of his tenets was to keep the city's standard of living within its income. (When questioned by a *Sarasota Herald* reporter what he does all day, Thompson responded with his dry wit: "Sit here and say no.")

Ever the hard worker, Thompson, who described himself as a workaholic, quickly familiarized himself with his responsibilities. He was said to be "delighted" with his new position, earning praise from an appreciative city

Rebirth

At his desk at the old city hall in the Hover Arcade on the downtown bay front. During the slow summer months, a city staffer could fish from the office window, provided Thompson was out of the office. *Jim Jennigan Photography, courtesy Barbara Thompson.*

commission. Mayor Robertson said, "Thompson's services have been highly satisfactory. We are most fortunate in having a man of his capabilities at this critical time."

Vice-Mayor Ben Drymon offered that the city could not have found a better man anywhere.

At the end of his first year, the *Herald* reported that Thompson "apparently found the formula for successful Sarasota municipal managership."

John Fite Robertson wrote, "His training, knowledge and experience had been of inestimable value to the city."

In turn, Thompson praised the city commission, saying, "It is a privilege to serve a community that wants good government and elects outstanding citizens to its Commission. I have had wonderful cooperation and support from city personnel and excellent relations with the Commission."

Operating out of a nondescript office at city hall, Thompson, though constantly busy, still offered an open door policy to both the public and city personnel. His phone number was listed in the directory.

He was quoted in the *Sarasota Herald* as saying that the citizens were, in effect, customers and the city's job was to satisfy those customers: "If we

The Rise of Sarasota

Thompson standing before a map of Sarasota shortly after he arrived to take up his duties in 1950. *Courtesy Barbara Thompson.*

Rebirth

A late 1940s shot of the old city hall building when it was located in the Hover Arcade at the foot of Lower Main Street. The sign points the way to the Lido Casino on Lido Beach but was later taken down as it confused tourists who thought the casino was through the archway. This was the site of Thompson's first office. *Sarasota County History Center, Pete Esthus Collection.*

want to attract the right type of customers, we must give them good drinking water, sanitary sewers, excellent police and fire protection, libraries and all the other things they have been used to in the communities from which they came." Always composed, he dealt with citizen complaints in an informal and precise manner.

He hired competent personnel and expected them to carry out their duties at the same high standard he set for himself. As he put it, his job was not to do everything but to hire qualified people who could handle their respective duties on their own. He allowed his subordinates the leeway to do their jobs but kept a watchful eye.

He came to rely heavily on his secretary, Mrs. Elizabeth Jackson, who was with him for twenty-five years before she retired. Thompson called her more of an administrative assistant than a secretary. She handled many of the public relations issues regarding both the public and the internal relations with other city employees. He did not know of anyone who could do the job better.

She worked for Thompson at both the old and new city halls and told reporter Dorothy Stockbridge of the *Sarasota Journal* that while she liked the functionality of the new office in the center of town, at the old one "I could look out the office and see the water. You couldn't beat the view."

As Thompson recalled, in the days of his arrival, there was not one traffic light operating in the city. The sole traffic signal in town was atop the American Legion War Memorial, and it was turned off during the war years. He switched it back on.

In a wish list to Santa in 1952, he wrote, "Dear Santa Claus, Please send me some new streets, a causeway, a fire station or two, some fire engines and police car, a new City Hall, an addition to the library and a dog pound, and I will be forever grateful. Sincerely, City Manager."

All of these wishes would be granted—in due time.

The year 1952 was an auspicious one in Sarasota's history; the community was fifty years old. On October 14, 1902, fifty-three men had voted to incorporate and elected John Hamilton Gillespie as the town's first mayor, along with councilmen J.B. Turner, Dr. J.O. Brown, George W. Blackburn, W.J. Hill and Harry L. Higel.

Sarasota's weeklong birthday celebration was a suitably festive affair, with doings at the Municipal Auditorium, a grand parade that went from the city hall building on Gulfstream Avenue along the length of Main Street, a pioneer dinner, a play (*Of These Sands*), a city-wide fiftieth-anniversary sale, a Pioneers Picnic and a costume ball.

An anniversary brochure touched on the past, touted the ongoing progress of the city and spoke of a bright future. Beneath a picture of the city's first mayor, A.B. Edwards, shaking hands with current mayor John Early, it was noted, "The torch of faith in Sarasota's future, held high since the city's beginning, burns even brighter today."

At the beginning of the 1950s, one of Sarasota's most pressing needs was the implementation of the water/sewer project, and one of Thompson's first duties was to participate in the adoption of the $3,750,000 city sewer/water system resolution and oversee its successful completion.

No small task. In the early 1900s, the stench from sewage that ran into Sarasota Bay was becoming intolerable. According to historian Karl Grismer, Dr. Jack Halton appeared before the town council to complain that the lack of sewers was a disgrace, noting that the smell from the Belle Haven Inn, the community's main hotel, was so bad that he could not finish eating a meal.

Rebirth

That prodded the council to warn the hotel to either provide cesspools or close down. It was not yet ready to levy taxes to build a sewage system.

More complaints about the odor downtown followed. At Five Points, the Sarasota House also reeked, causing its owner, major landowner and developer J.H. Lord, to install pipes from the hotel, through alleys and into the bay.

By 1911, most townspeople were sufficiently fed up with the problem, and after a hardscrabble battle between the progressives of the community and those who were satisfied with the status quo, they finally voted fifty-seven for and thirty-five against a $20,000 bond for building a water/sewer system. Once passed, Sarasota could move forward.

But although the sewer line extended four hundred feet away from town, the discharge still ended up in Sarasota Bay.

Sarasota could not move forward and capture its share of Florida newcomers with this antiquated sewage system, not to mention its effect on the bay.

Thompson oversaw the construction of the new water/sewer system. Completed in 1951, it doubled the city's water capacity, offered 115 sewer lines to four thousand homes and businesses, included ten pump houses and treated the sewage at a newly constructed plant, thereby preventing thousands of gallons of raw sewage from flowing into Sarasota Bay.

When the system was ready, the *Herald* ran an article, along with a picture of the new facility, with the headline "Sanitary System Enhances Future." It noted, "Thus as the city enters its thirty-first year as a county seat, a progressive west coast leader and a nationally known year-round resort, it does so with two new modern municipal systems both planned to expand with the city's continued growth."

Throughout the decade of the 1950s, a spirit of optimism not seen since the heady days of the 1920s was evident. Glowing newspaper stories covered new developments, businesses opening and construction of schools and churches. Building records were being set and reset. The valuation of properties subject to tax assessment increased almost 50 percent from 1949 to 1953, going from $50,201,410 to $74,482,000.

Building permits shot up from 3,634 issued in 1949–50, with building valuations of $8,568,826, to 4,244 permits with valuations of $10,185,632 during the 1952–53 cycle.

And while city projects such as the new water/sewer system were an obvious and welcomed necessity for Sarasota's growth to continue, two other events—the moving of the American Legion War Memorial from the center of Five Points to Gulfstream Avenue and the removal of the memorial oak trees that lined Main Street from Orange Avenue east past the courthouse—engendered controversy.

Sarasota was very obviously changing, and while most favored the transformation—the developers, builders, businesspeople, store owners, bankers, chamber of commerce and city commissioners—not everyone was in agreement. Some were satisfied with the status quo, thank you very much, and throughout the decade they fought back against projects that they saw as redefining the ambiance of their community. Thompson welcomed growth, but it had to be planned.

As one of the city commissioners summed up the tree situation: "It is unfortunate that the trees have to make way for progress, but it appears that we can't have both."

He was referencing the removal of the memorial oak trees, one planted for each serviceman who served in World War I and dedicated in 1922. They lined both sides of Main Street from Orange Avenue past the courthouse, and that section of the street was renamed Victory Avenue.

Some remembered the July day in 1922 when the trees, then mere seedlings, were dedicated by Woman's Club president Mrs. Frederick H. Guenther promising Sarasota's servicemen that their memorial was an avenue of living trees whose beauty and grateful shade would delight and bless generations long after they had passed on.

Ken Thompson echoed the commissioner's assertion that they were hindering progress, stating, "The presence of trees along Main Street has undoubtedly curtailed development of the city's main street as a business street." Local store owners agreed, and after a hard-fought campaign led by a group formed to protect the trees called Friends of Friendly Oaks, they ended up being chopped down a few at a time.

Each time one was removed, it was written up in the paper. An editorial in *The News* called their removal the "Bitter Fruits of Progress."

The removal of the American Legion War Memorial, which had been in the center of Five Points since 1928, was less controversial. While a bid to relocate it from the very heart of downtown Sarasota was defeated by public outrage in 1937, in 1954, the State Road Department declared it a traffic hazard, and with very little protest, it was moved to Gulfstream Avenue and rededicated in today's Reverend J.D. Hamel Park.

Rebirth

One of the casualties of the modern era was the removal of the American Legion War Memorial from the center of Five Points, where it had stood since 1928 as a visible reminder of Sarasota's contribution to the war effort. In 1954, the statue was rolled down Lower Main Street to Gulfstream Avenue and placed in today's Reverend J.D. Hamel Park, where its presence is less visible. *Sarasota County History Center, Bill Blackstone Collection.*

Inscribed with the names of Sarasotans fallen in battle, it serves as the focal point for Memorial Day, Veterans' Day and Fourth of July celebrations.

As today, not everyone was enthused with the new system of government and tried to change it. During this era, the names of prospective commissioners were put forward by a Citizens' Committee of local businessmen and civic leaders who favored the commission/manager form of government. George Higgins, who discovered Thompson, was a prominent member of this group.

But in 1951, two Independents, John Early and Forrest Freeman, actively campaigned and ran against the committee choices. Another candidate, Ralph Correll, was endorsed by the committee but had been nominated by an independent group. His would be the deciding vote if there were a vote along partisan lines. The paper noted that there had been quite a bit of haranguing among the commission members.

The *Tampa Tribune* reported:

> *Early, an old line politician, made it clear after being selected mayor that he thought the mayor could exercise a lot of power. It is apparent that he is gradually finding out that the city manager is actually the head of the city with Commissioners to enact the ordinances and keep an eye on the operation of the city. Early has learned that it was the City Manager, not himself who had the authority to handle a question or matter.*

For the 1952 election, the Sarasota Citizens Committee put forward Ben H. Hopkins Jr., a local automobile dealer, to go against the Independent candidate, and he won handily by nearly a two-to-one majority. He was chosen to be vice-mayor.

With Early, Freeman and Correll often voting together against Hopkins and Farrell, what *Herald* reporter Irv Edelson called the most controversial reign in the history of the city manager/commission form of government occurred at the end of 1952 and the beginning of 1953 with an attempt to oust the chief of police, Robert Wilson, and after that, some speculated, the city manager.

In December, Early announced that an investigation was going to be conducted. Spurious rumors were circulating that the chief had been seen drunk in public and that he was inefficient in carrying out his duties.

This was before Government in the Sunshine; secret meetings were held, and according to the *Herald*, two reporters took turns listening to the meeting from a hiding place in the rafters and published the goings-on.

The *Herald* reported that there was a faction in the police department trying to discredit the chief and his administration because they had been passed over for promotion in favor of Wilson.

On April 6, 1953, Correll, Early and Freeman voted to relieve the chief. At the next commission meeting, "an irate public" gathered at city hall and demanded that a recall petition of the commissioners be distributed.

Rebirth

This was all headline material in the *Herald*, which agreed with the recall of the commissioners, editorializing: "Let the People Speak!"

The paper noted, "These three commissioners have sniped at city employees and at the basic principles of this City Manager form of government, so as to create a situation in which the people must now choose whether they wish administration according to the spirit of the city charter, or a return to personal, politically dictated government." It branded the firing of Wilson "arbitrary."

A petition was hand delivered to Mayor Early's home with 175 names protesting the ouster of Wilson, who was a hardworking police chief and well respected in the community.

Photographs were run in the paper showing long lines of people signing commissioner recall petitions at Five Points and disgruntled citizens packing the commission chambers.

The paper reported that within an hour and forty minutes, four hundred names had been gathered.

Succumbing to community pressure, on April 9, Early changed his mind and voted with Hopkins and Ferrell to reinstate Wilson. Correll abstained, and Freeman voted against the motion.

Wilson was vindicated and put back on the job on April 9, but the recall of the three commissioners went forward.

On April 20, Early said that he had intended to leave the commission due to his poor health and that due to the "increased tension" he decided to resign. He denied reports that he was not in favor of the commission/manager form of government. He was replaced by Le Roy Fenne, and the commissioner recall movement petered out.

Shortly thereafter, Correll suffered a heart attack and died in office on June 9.

As the county of Sarasota continued to grow, it became evident that the public would be better served if Sarasota Municipal Hospital was placed under the control of the Sarasota County District Hospital Board, a move that relieved the city of financing the hospital, shifting the burden to the county.

The switch became official at midnight on July 1, 1954, and the hospital became Sarasota Memorial Hospital. Reflecting the area's increased population, three floors were being added to it, with two more expected to be completed by 1955.

Thompson, always looking for ways to save the city money, lauded the move, stating, "Last Tuesday's favorable vote for additional bonds for the hospital...signifies the public's desire not only to have excellent facilities, but by inference reaffirms their concurrence in being consolidated in a larger county-wide authority."

One of Thompson's guiding principles was cost. Early in his administration, he indicated his philosophy: "To relate all action to the fundamental of performing the most municipal services of the highest quality for the fewest tax dollars."

July 1, 1954, also saw the start of construction of the city's new Community House. Designed by noted architects Ralph and William Zimmerman, the facility was located behind the Chidsey Library adjacent to the Civic Center. It was to be used primarily as a youth center for dances, games and general get-togethers. Fifteen hundred persons came to the opening reception and annual Christmas dance for teenagers on December 20, 1954.

Another major nod to progress and modernization occurred in October 1954. At a celebratory event that was billed as Sarasota's Diamond Jubilee of Light, thousands filled downtown to watch as the city switched from incandescent to fluorescent lights. A dance at Five Points followed.

On the night of October 26, the old streetlights were turned off by A.B. Edwards, and after a brief blackout, Ben Hopkins III, the five-year-old son of Mayor Ben Hopkins Jr., threw the switch for the new system, "illuminating Main Street in all its fluorescent glory."

The event was timed to coincide with Thomas Edison's invention of the incandescent bulb.

In 1953, Charles H. Pickett, treasurer and tax collector, reported a 49 percent increase in the tax assessment roll since 1949. With the rampant growth and profound changes came comparisons to the free-wheeling Florida boom of the '20s, but with Ken Thompson at the helm, the vagaries associated with those days were unlikely in Sarasota. One of his tenets was to "develop an atmosphere of unhurried management."

Credit was given to him by the *Sarasota Herald*, which reported, "Sarasota's orderly and rapid growth is due to its present City Manager as much as to

Rebirth

the efforts of any one man...He has been one of the major architects in the building of this city ever since."

Quoting from John W. Bloomer, managing editor of the *Sarasota Herald*, in an article that appeared in the *Evening Gazette* of Worcester, Massachusetts, "[The postwar boom] hit Florida with the result that the population has almost doubled in the succeeding six years and residential and commercial construction program in excess of $30,000,000 has been carried out." He noted that the increases could have "led to a status of near civic and financial chaos."

Bloomer reported that thanks in no small measure to the policies of Ken Thompson, "the reverse is true in Sarasota. The city's financial condition is the best that it has been in 30 years and rapid strides are being made toward retiring the large bonded debt hanging over the community from the boom of the Twenties."

The News, an afternoon daily, assured, "Everything indicates that real estate in Florida is no longer a speculative venture. There is slim chance that the current boom will collapse into another sensational bust."

When Thompson's salary was raised to $12,000 in 1952, a *Sarasota Herald* editorial indicated that he would be worth two or three times that amount and spelled out exactly what the manager of the city of Sarasota, the "biggest business in town," did:

> *He is responsible for the city's daily operations and services which will cost $975,000 during the next fiscal year.*
> *He is responsible for the operations of the sewer-water system, which has a budget of $485,700 for next year.*
> *He is responsible for the municipal hospital and its $460,000 budget for 1952–'53.*
> *He is responsible for the new water shop, and its $227,000 budget.*
> *He is responsible for the $250,000 budget of the city shops and garage.*
> *He is responsible for the $140,000 Trailer Park operations, the $101,000 at Bobby Jones Golf Course, $47,800 of the parking meter fund and $42,000 at Lido Beach.*
> *Then there is the $322,050 in the debt service fund.*

The editorial also mentioned that like the chief of police and the fire chief, he was on duty twenty-four hours a day, seven days a week, and four hundred city employees looked to him for guidance and advice.

He was called one of the busiest people in Sarasota. Just two years after coming to Sarasota, his talents were recognized by his peers throughout

The Rise of Sarasota

Florida when he was voted president of the Florida City and County Managers Association.

Street improvement—widening, resurfacing, renaming and rerouting—was a major goal for the city in the early 1950s.

Until 1959, U.S. Highway 41 ran along Main Street, which ended at Gulfstream Avenue. Connecting Broadway Avenue (the North Tamiami Trail) to Gulfstream Avenue would offer newcomers driving through town an opportunity to view beautiful Sarasota Bay and, hopefully, entice them to stay.

According to the Polk City Directory, in 1955 the Sarasota Police Department, under the leadership of Chief Robert N. Wilson, was described as a modern, efficient department with twenty-six uniformed personnel, police staff and four patrol cars equipped with two-way FM radio. The crime rate in Sarasota was said to be one of the lowest in the United States. During this time, the police station was located on State Street, until it moved to Ringling Boulevard in 1959. Thompson said of Wilson that his work was "outstanding."
Sarasota County History Center, Bill Blackstone Collection.

Rebirth

The extension, which predated the four-lane highway, cost $8,000 and was completed in 1951, and as the *Sarasota Herald* put it, "this short stretch of road is a long piece of promotion for Sarasota...And as soon as more folks realize what we've got in this town and make the effort to show it off more smartly, business will boom more than ever."

Two years later, calls to rename many Sarasota streets gathered steam. Roads with duplicate names were scattered throughout the city. There were four Oak Streets in all different parts of Sarasota. Police and Fire Department responders likened some emergency calls to trying to find a needle in a haystack.

In May 1953, the new system, confusing at first to some, went into effect. An educational booklet listing the new streets and new house numbers next to the old was offered, and the switch was timed to occur when the new phone books came out.

By April 1954, Thompson reported to the commission that the resurfacing program carried out with proceeds of a $1 million bond issue was nearly 80 percent complete. He requested another $100,000 a year for two years to complete the repaving of all streets in the city.

Other road improvements included the widening of the North and South Tamiami Trail and adding flourescent streetlights along the trail, to be completed in 1957.

The average length of stay for a city manager in the mid-'50s was five years, and Thompson and his wife celebrated this milestone by taking the members of the first city commission that had hired him, along with their wives, to dinner at the Colony Restaurant on Harding Circle as a token of their gratitude.

Always dressed in a shirt and tie and usually a jacket while at city hall, and sometimes wearing a golfer's hat, Thompson managed to unwind in his free time by sailing and flying, both of which he loved. Later, he would take up art, becoming proficient in wire art.

Keeping in tip-top shape also helped shred stress, and after he quit jogging, he took up the trampoline and was quite proficient at it.

One of Thompson's great pleasures was flying over the city on Saturday mornings, pointing out to whoever was with him, often a commissioner, the changes that were occurring in Sarasota and sharing

The Rise of Sarasota

One of Thompson's favorite pastimes was flying, which he learned to do in Miami Beach. Commissioners were often taken aloft for a bird's-eye view of Sarasota. *Courtesy Barbara Thompson.*

his visions of the city's future and the best course of action to take to ensure proper growth.

After the flight, it was usually a fried chicken lunch and more city talk at the Ranch House restaurant near the airport.

Thompson's unflappable coolness under fire was legendary, and his second wife, Barbara, related an incident that underscored this. They were flying over the Gulf of Mexico when the engine on his plane quit cold. Without a trace of panic, Thompson matter-of-factly asked her to reach in the glove compartment and find a map so he could search for an emergency landing site. She was terrified at first but was calmed by Thompson's matter-of-fact request. What seemed like eternity to her, and a brief ho-hum to him, ended when the engine restarted and they continued on their journey.

Rebirth

The *Sarasota Herald* reported that, among his early successes, he had been responsible for helping to develop land control regulations for subdivisions that were adopted in 1953 governing street paving, curbs, gutters, drainage, water and sewage, as well as compatibility of the new development with the surrounding area. He was applauded for being a moving force in bolstering the zoning ordinances that would prevent the miscues of the '20s.

He called the ongoing growth of Sarasota a distinct challenge. In a *Sarasota Herald* article, he was quoted as saying, "It is a challenge that I welcome—a challenge to my ability to administer policies that the Commission will adopt for the future to keep us in the forefront of Florida Cities."

To him, letting tomorrow take care of tomorrow's problem was the "antithesis of planning." To sell the idea of planning, he advocated planning moderately at first and then, as it proved its value, "intensify it."

Planning would preclude the vagaries of the previous real estate boom.

As Flory remembered, developers of days gone by "gave no thought to drainage, utilities or other improvements. They laid out four lots to the acre and would sell off each of these lots for the price originally paid for the acre, and they left the city holding the bag as far as any improvements were concerned."

For Thompson, the new subdivisions that were springing up in rural areas needed a high standard of control. "Cheap land rises in value, and therefore, should bear the cost of adornments." He likened the improvements to a new subdivision to "requiring a country cousin to buy a new suit before you let him join your family circle."

His theory: "Rural land on being admitted to the urban family should be required to qualify for urbanity at its own expense prior to admittance...A high standard of subdivision control encourages a higher investment in improvements."

Unlike the boom days that Flory and Edwards recalled, under Thompson's watch, the city would *not* be left holding the bag as far as subdivision improvements were concerned, and most assuredly, taxpayers would *not* be squeezed dry by speculators.

The driving force of Sarasota's earlier growth spurt was making fast money by turning over property quickly for a profit, much as the condo and home flippers of recent days.

An advertisement from the Roaring Twenties asked, "How Does Your Brain Work?" and assured readers that unless they acted quickly, purchased quickly and resold quickly, they would surely lose out on the moneymaking potential inherent in Sarasota real estate.

During the mid-'20s, the newspapers were filled with full-page ads underscoring the notion that it was easy to profit from Sarasota property: "Values Are Constantly Enhancing." "An Opportunity for Big Profit." "Price Climbing, Let Your Profits Go Up with the Climb."

Some lots sold repeatedly, rising in price with each sale. A property on Golden Gate Point sold seven times. In 1925, the *Herald* reported an increase in property sales of 1000 percent over 1924.

Then, with the bust at the end of 1926 tied to the September hurricane that devastated Miami, Sarasota fell on bleak economic times. Taxes could not be collected, the infrastructure deteriorated, newcomers quit coming and Sarasota, with the rest of Florida, fell into a depression that worsened with the Great Depression of the 1930s.

By contrast, post–World War II developments were advertised as places to live, raise a family and enjoy life, not a moneymaking opportunity to buy quickly, sell quickly and move on.

Throughout his tenure, Thompson was often quoted in the press saying that he merely carried out the policy wishes of the commission, which was elected by the people of Sarasota. And Mayor Ben Hopkins underscored this, remarking that if the people of Sarasota who spread rumors that the commissioners were puppets of the city manager knew the real story, they would be surprised at the number of times there were differences of opinion.

Indeed, during these years, the Sarasota City Commission was generally composed of successful merchants and businessmen, well known in the community, which they served without compensation. What was good for Sarasota was good for them, and they were motivated to make Sarasota the best that it could be. Often, they were active members of the chamber of commerce and the area service clubs. This was still a very close-knit community; business could be and was conducted with a handshake.

Rebirth

The *Sarasota Herald* gave Thompson his due for the progress the city was continuing to make:

> *For if any one man deserves a boost for the condition of Sarasota, it is City Manager Kenneth Thompson...The city has been "rocking and rolling" under Thompson's guiding hands. City Commissioners have respected the City Manager's judgment and Thompson in turn has adopted a "hands off" attitude on matters of policy—unless asked to express his opinion.*

Hopkins said the city could be proud of its city manager and hoped he would remain into the distant future.

Transportation is a key ingredient for a successful tourist-oriented community. At the turn of the previous century, when Sarasota residents learned that train service was coming to their little village, they voted to incorporate as a town, expecting that an influx of newcomers was in the offing.

During the 1920s land boom, local roads were improved, and highways were constructed to allow easier access to the Sunshine State, with cities improving their roads and competing with one another to lure the newcomers.

In 1927, Sarasota was finally linked to Tampa and Miami when the Tamiami Trail was completed.

And while automobile travel is still the primary means of entry into Sarasota, air travel long ago replaced the train as the transport of choice.

Sarasota had been served by two railroad companies: the Seaboard Air Line and the Atlantic Coast Line. As train travel tapered off, the two merged, becoming the Seaboard Coast Line Railroad, using the station at Main Street and Lemon Avenue. The Spanish-Mission Atlantic Coast Line station at the eastern terminus of Main Street was turned into a Brewmaster's Restaurant and was demolished in 1986 despite the city's effort to save it. The razing was derided by Thompson.

Today's SRQ International Airport began as a Works Progress Administration project in the late 1930s, and when World War II broke out, it was used as a training base for the Army Air Force, first for bombers and then for fighter planes.

By the mid-'50s, it was looking the worse for wear. The terminal certainly was not in keeping with Sarasota's new image of a modern, thriving city,

Construction underway for the new Sarasota-Bradenton Airport, designed by the renowned architect Paul Rudolph, who did a lot of work locally, including Riverview High School and the new addition to Sarasota High School. He would go on to become the chairman of the Yale School of Architecture. *Sarasota County History Center.*

and the Sarasota-Manatee Airport Authority approved construction of a new facility.

Plans for the new terminal were from Paul Rudolph, the great modernist of the Sarasota School of Architecture, who would go on to become the world-renowned dean of the Yale School of Architecture. The project was expected to cost $450,000, with some of the funding coming from the federal government and the rest through a bond issue.

Ground for the terminal was broken on August 15, 1958, and while the original plans were scaled back due to monetary considerations, the new terminal, dedicated on October 25, 1959, reflected a progressive city and, with some additions, served the area's needs until 1989, when the current SRQ International Airport facility was opened.

Rebirth

Even with the growth and infrastructure improvements, the Sarasota of 1955 still had much in common with its past. It was still the Circus City, headquarters of the Ringling Bros. and Barnum & Bailey Circus, the top tourist attraction in Florida. The first John Ringling Bridge was still in operation, stretching from Golden Gate Point, usually lined with fishermen and showing its years. Bird Key was a small island, occupied by only the Worcester Mansion. Sarasota Bay lapped all the way up to Gulfstream Avenue, and downtown still filled all the needs of the community and its guests.

For the most part, the beaches were undeveloped tropical paradises, and tourists were lodged mostly in downtown hotels, apartments and boardinghouses. Both the North and South Trail began filling up with motels.

But during the next five years, dramatic and far-reaching changes would take place as Sarasota continued to grow and modernize.

By the end of the decade, the circus would be gone, U.S. 41 would be rerouted through Luke Wood Park and along the bay front, the Arvida Corporation would come to town to develop the keys and there would be another attempt to oust the city manager.

In 1952, the Ringling interests presented a plan to the commission to fill the submerged lands around Bird Key for a high-class housing development, a real boon to the tax base when completed.

A proposal submitted by them two years earlier had not been well received by the commission or the general public, who were concerned that it would detract from the beauty of Sarasota Bay. But their scaled-down version seemed acceptable to individual commissioners. Thompson informed the commission that the plan, by Ralph and William Zimmerman and revised over the years, would be good for the city.

Approval was expected to be given at the commission meeting on September 24, 1952. But the deal breaker that evening involved Coolidge Park, a 1,200-foot-long and, at its widest, 200-foot-wide sliver of sand that the public used for beach purposes.

No mention was made of the park at the previous meeting, and when the developers were told they had to relinquish any claim to it, they balked.

Former governor Doyle Carlton, representing the developers, told the commission that if giving up Coolidge Park was a condition, "The whole works is out."

Other proposals were submitted, and the Zimmerman plan was finally approved but never implemented. During the process, there were some acrimonious exchanges.

At a public hearing, an irate congressman, James Haley, blasted the notion proffered by a member of the Ringling group that a commission member opposed the project because of a feud with some of the Ringling family. Haley shot, "What do you mean coming here with this curbside gossip! You can't come down here and tell us how to run our affairs. Why don't you go back to New York and run your own business?"

In the end, the development of Bird Key would have to wait until 1959 and the arrival of Arthur Vining Davis and the Arvida Corp., which bought out the Ringling holdings.

The continued improvement of area roads and bridges was always high on the to-do list of Thompson and the commission. Enter the State Road Department. Its solution to ease the flow of traffic was to four-lane the highways and reroute Highway U.S. 41 along the downtown bay front as a bypass and, concurrently, replace the aging John Ringling Bridge with a four-lane version.

To accomplish the controversial plan, it became necessary to take a swath of land through the center of beautiful Luke Wood Park, and a large area between Gulfstream Avenue and the bay needed to be dredged and filled to accommodate the new highway—Bay Front Drive.

Critics of the plan put forward by Al Rogero, point man for the State Road Board, abounded.

Of the Luke Wood Park loss, Betty Burket wrote colorfully in her Roundabout column in *The News*, that it was "a deed so ugly that it will remain like a welt across the minds of our people for decades to come."

The design of the new intersection joining Highways 41 and 301 was faulted for bringing together "too many points of conflicting traffic."

The *Sarasota Herald* said its design would confuse motorists.

Rebirth

Construction finally started in late 1957. Property owners along Gulfstream Avenue who claimed riparian rights to the land at the bay front sought an injunction.

The case ultimately ended with a settlement in August 1959, with the city reportedly paying $75,000 to $100,000 in compensation to the landowners.

As the project took shape in 1958, it was harshly criticized by members of the Institute of Architects, who were holding their regional conference in Sarasota that April.

Douglas Haskell, editor of the *Architectural Forum*, ridiculed the proposal, saying, among other things, that it was "unforgivable and idiotic, cutting off the community from the bay front."

Architect Paul Rudolph disliked the new highway because it separated the city from the water, its greatest asset.

The regional engineer for the U.S. Bureau of Roads, Rex S. Anderson, reacted to Haskell's scathing denunciation, saying he was "astounded to find such local dissatisfaction."

"I thought it was widely acclaimed," Anderson said.

Many did favor it, including the chamber of commerce, which liked the idea of showcasing Sarasota's crown jewel, the downtown bay front, to passing motorists, which was the whole point of the exercise.

Plans to beautify the area around city hall at the old Hover Arcade, now in the middle of a major roadway, an island of yesterday surrounded by a concrete sea of today, were submitted by architect William Zimmerman, who had argued for better city planning.

Zimmerman hoped to turn the building's grounds into "a Spanish type oasis," refurbishing its exterior, adding serpentine streams of water along both sides and placing an amphitheater around the Memorial Flagpole on Gulfstream Avenue.

But its days were numbered. It was declared unsafe in 1956 by the City Planning Board, which recommended an examination of the structure. At that time, Zimmerman warned that among the issues, the building had only one exit, and if a fire broke out it would be disastrous.

Chairman of the Planning Board Ben Drymon agreed that a new facility was necessary but did not feel the city was financially able to demolish the old and construct a new one at the present time.

The original road/bridge plan by the state was a $7 million package deal that called for the replacement of the original Ringling Causeway, while adding a new two-lane bridge over Big Pass that would link Lido Key and Siesta Key. Each bridge was slated to charge a ten-cent toll.

Thompson stirs up some "rosin potatoes" while noted architect William Zimmerman, of the Sarasota School of Architecture, and Dallas Dort, local rancher and one of the founders of the New College of Sarasota, look on. *Courtesy Barbara Thompson.*

Rebirth

Interested citizens filled the Municipal Auditorium to hear the proposal and reacted strongly against the toll. The toll was shelved, as was the bridge over Big Pass. Of the latter, civic leader Karl Bickel said, "The Big Pass scheme which replaces the Twelfth Street location is the mystery. Apparently it was created in the dark, fostered in silence and handed to the State Road Board and through it to the people of Sarasota like a bright new bomb."

The new highway and the new Ringling Bridge, which was moved from its former starting point on Golden Gate Point, were completed in 1959.

In the mid-'50s, two events came together to increase the comfort factor of Sarasota and make it more appealing: air conditioning and the unrelenting war on mosquitoes.

The upturn in in-home air conditioners was due to shopping in air-conditioned stores and working in air-conditioned offices. People began demanding the same cool surroundings in their homes and cars, and manufacturers responded by developing low-cost air-conditioning systems. Soon all new homes would come with central air or at least window units.

As for mosquitoes, they were more than an irritant. They traveled in black swarms, always preventing pleasant summertime outdoor evenings. And while residents had put up with them as part of life in Sarasota, they were hampering summer tourism, and they would have to go.

Mel Williams was appointed director of mosquito control for Sarasota County in December 1945, and using fogger jeeps and airplanes, he and his men sprayed with DDT, chlordane and malathion in what was called Operation Mosquito and the Dawn Patrol.

In the end, Williams and his crew finally got control of the problem and probably did as much as any person to increase the enjoyment of the summer tourist and long-suffering residents.

By 1956, Sarasota was reportedly the fastest-growing city in the nation on a percentage basis. A Babson population poll indicated an increase of 108 percent since 1950.

THE RISE OF SARASOTA

City commissioners superimposed over a photograph of the bay front, 1956, at a time when mayors and commissioners were unpaid. Their reward was community appreciation for a job well done. *Sarasota County History Center.*

An article in *The News* noted that in 1956 Sarasota had a $93,000,000 tax roll and was a $4,141,890-a-year business enterprise. Indicating that more than half the cities in the United States with a population of between twenty-five and forty thousand were governed by the commissioner/manager system, it noted the benefits of the system: "Sarasota is outstanding in its physical cleanliness and beauty and is outstanding, too in its cleanliness of government. From the mayor-commissioner down to the newest rookie cop, Sarasota is a model of good government in action."

Tourism was increasing even during the usually slow summer months. According to *The News*, among the sixty-seven counties in Florida, Sarasota County placed tenth in the total number of retail service establishments and their total receipts.

To accommodate the influx of newcomers, the number of lodging rooms between 1946 and 1956 increased from 5,475 to 13,471, the number of

Rebirth

restaurants increased from 126 with a seating capacity of 5,251 to 300 with a capacity of 15,963 and bank deposits shot from $18,667,338 to $115,162,091.

Large-scale housing developments were popping up throughout the city and county, as were shopping centers, schools, churches, strip centers and trailer parks, which replaced orange groves and pastureland.

Martin Paver and his sons Paul and Stanley formed Paver Construction Company and became a leader in local housing developments with Paver Park followed by Kensington Park.

In short order, other developments offered low-cost, moderately priced and high-end homes: Greenbriar Estates and Melody Heights, "Where Your Life Will Always Be a Song." The massive Roland S. King–Frank Smith Southgate project advertised, "Where You Live Among the Orange Blossoms."

At the upper end of the housing scale, Lido Shores, Harbor Acres, Cherokee Park and numerous others all followed the new guidelines set down by Thompson and his planners at city hall.

The election of December 1957 might have led to the dismissal of Thompson.

In the largest voter turnout in Sarasota history, the citizens voted into office three members of the Independent Taxpayer Association, electing to the commission Frank Hoersting, Frederic W. Dennis and Jack L. Turner, defeating the Sarasota Citizens League candidates Frank Conrad, Clement Ferrell and Weston Burquest Sr.

Hoersting was named mayor, replacing outgoing A. Ray Howard. The three newcomers joined John O. Binns and Eddie Marable. Hoersting's victory was all the sweeter for him because he had run independently five previous times, losing in 1956 by only sixty-nine votes.

Once again, speculation was rife that with this mandate, the Independents, endorsed by *The News*, a Republican-leaning paper, now with a voting majority, would oust some of the top administrators in city government, including Thompson.

Thompson assured the public that he would not resign. He told a reporter for the *Tampa Tribune* that he had no intention of deserting the people of Sarasota.

But instead of the friction and head rolling that was expected, the five commissioners from the two factions promised cooperation and harmony.

Binns, now in the minority, said he could see no reason why they could not all do what was best for Sarasota.

For his part, the new mayor avowed, "Contrary to the opinion of many we did not come to wreck the city nor to roll any heads but to help build the city as we know how. We come with the spirit of cooperation for the loyal employees of the city."

In a joint statement, the three winners said, "We make one promise—good, clean, open, and above board government for all." The election, they said, brought democracy to the city.

As for the rumor that Ken Thompson might be fired, Hoersting offered, "We think the world of the City Manager Ken Thompson, City Clerk L.B. Ashley, City Treasurer Charles H. Pickett and their employees and are proud to be a part of that team."

In his farewell speech, outgoing mayor Howard said of Thompson:

> *It has been a great privilege to have worked with City Manager Kenneth Thompson. His knowledge of the many phases of municipal government and his ability to analyze and interpret them to us has been invaluable... And as sincerely as I know how, I hope he serves Sarasota for many more years to come.*

Summing up Sarasota's progress over the past year, Howard noted the widening of the North Trail; the beginning of the Bay Front Drive/Ringling Causeway project, which he indicated would be accomplished with $6 million in state funds and only $1 million locally; a $75,000 pool for Newtown; and improved city services.

January 10, 1959, was a historic day. The new Ringling Bridge and Causeway was ready to be opened—a day for which many had waited a long time. On hand for the dedication was James A. Morton, the engineer hired by John Ringling to build the first bridge, which opened in February 1926.

Ringling built the bridge to allow automobile transportation to Ringling Isles, his and Owen Burns's development on Lido Key. He had brought the colorful Czecho-Slovakian Band to town to add excitement to the event, and they gave free concerts from a band shell built for them on St. Armands and at another one on Palm Avenue.

Rebirth

Until the end of the 1950s, U.S. Highway 41 ran along Main Street, and service stations lined the way to accommodate travelers passing through town. This Standard Oil Station at Main Street and Osprey Avenue was opened in 1935 and operated by Elmer "Al" Tegenkamp. In 1952, Ralph W. Reese bought it, and it has been in the Reese family for three generations, operated now by Rick Reese, who took it over from his father, Dick. It's the last full-service station standing on Main Street in downtown Sarasota. It's also the last station that will clean your windshield, put air in your tires and check your oil. *Sarasota County History Center.*

Hourly bus transportation was scheduled to and from the Ringling headquarters on Main Street. Before the day was over, thousands from all over the state had poured onto the key to marvel at what the *Herald* called a "tropical Utopia of broad boulevards, canals, palm trees and alluring parkways."

It was reported that on that opening day, property sales exceeded $1 million.

In June 1927, the *Herald* trumpeted the news "Ringling Gives Causeway to City" and added, "There are no words adequate with which to express our appreciation for this wonderful donation."

Later, keeping the bridge repaired, especially after the real estate crash and the Great Depression, would be problematic.

Morton commented that Ringling's bridge was designed to last only twenty years and no more, and he was proud that it lasted fourteen years beyond that.

The Rise of Sarasota

The Worcester Mansion on Bird Key was located where the Bird Key Yacht Club is today. It was built by Thomas Worcester to be the retirement home for his wife, Davie. Sadly, she died before the home was completed. When John Ringling purchased Bird Key, the mansion was slated to be the Winter White House for Warren G. Harding, but Harding died before the plan could be carried out. For a number of years, Ida Ringling North, John's sister, lived there, until she passed away in 1950. *Sarasota County History Center.*

On hand for the dedication of the new bridge were state legislators, senators, local officials and hundreds of citizens who had followed the progress as they crossed over the old bridge.

It was a chilly, forty-degree morning that greeted the crowd who gathered to hear the speeches and watch the ribbon cutting. A fleet of cars from Horn's Cars of Yesterday led a procession across, preceded by the color guards of the American Legion and the Veterans of Foreign Wars, Sarasota High School Marching Band and majorettes. Sarasota mayor Frederic Dennis served as the master of ceremonies, and some of the speeches were abbreviated because of the chilly weather. The crowd was grateful.

Al Rogero, the key to making the project a reality, was on hand to present the bridge to local officials in the name of Governor LeRoy Collins. He congratulated the contractors and called the bridge a symbol of cooperation.

The next day, the banner headline on the *Sarasota Herald*: "City's Key Dream Becomes Concrete—Bridge Is Opened."

The new bridge, together with the Bay Front Highway, which allowed easy access to St. Armands, Lido Key and Longboat Key, typified modern Sarasota.

Rebirth

Looking west at Sarasota Bay, 1959, shortly after U.S. 41 was rerouted. Note that Bird Key had not yet been developed, and there are no high-rise condominiums downtown. *Robert J. Ford Photo, Sarasota County History Center.*

Equaling the importance of the new Ringling Causeway and Bay Front Drive for the community was the announcement that Arthur Vining Davis was coming to Sarasota with big plans for the keys.

His Arvida Corporation's development proposals for Bird Key and Longboat Key were to today's Sarasota what Andrew McAnsh's construction of the Mira Mar Apartments and Hotel had been to yesterday's version: a vehicle for attracting high-brow newcomers.

Arvida would take the vision of John Ringling and Owen Burns that was dashed with the 1926 real estate crash and make it a reality.

Over one thousand real estate people gathered in the Municipal Auditorium to listen to Arvida's vision of Sarasota's future. The immediate plan called for Bird Key to be expanded to make room for 511 homesites, 291 of which were to be on the waterfront and priced at $17,000 to $32,000. Interior lots sold for $9,000 to $15,000.

In a full-page advertisement, Arvida declared, "It's a rare city here or abroad that has an iota of the charm of Sarasota. You'll find us good neighbors."

Ed Hoyt, who was working with Thompson as his assistant when the Arvida plans were submitted and was later the Sarasota County administrator, indicated that when negotiations were going on, the Coastal Engineering Lab at the University of Florida was hired to study the project's effect on the bay bottom. Using a scale mock-up of Sarasota Bay, they were able to regulate currents, and by using dye they could see where the currents would flow. They determined that Arvida's Bird Key would not be harmful to the bay, except to the bottom grasses and the fish that lived there.

Hoyt conjectured that with all the regulations in place today, the Arvida plan would not be approved.

In his book *Sarasota and Me*, Don Smally, whose firm Smally Wellford & Nalven (SWN), a consulting, engineering and surveying firm that did a lot of business for both the city and the county, said that due to the loss of so much of the bay bottom to Bird Key, and to prevent further loss, a group was formed "with some prominent people including Sarasota City Commissioners Gil Waters and Ted Sperling and Mayor Sam Gibbons of Longboat Key."

And while nothing could be done about Bird Key, the group fought hard for the prevention of further filling of the bay bottoms.

Smally indicated that when Arvida was setting its sights on South Lido Key, Coon Key and Otter Key, "the City Commission, advised by Thompson, reacted by ordering the creation of a bulkhead line along all of the involved shoreline beyond which no filling or dredging could take place."

Arvida objected to the bulkhead and took the matter to court. Smally, who did a lot of testifying on the issue, said Arvida ended the battle by offering the property on South Lido for park purposes, thus creating South Lido Park, known today as Ted Sperling Park at South Lido Beach to honor Sperling for fighting the good fight for the protection of Sarasota's natural resources.

Sarasota ended 1959 with the largest construction year in its history up to that time, some $12,331,366 in new construction.

Rebirth

A relatively minor but noteworthy event occurred in February 1959 in segregated Sarasota when four black golfers showed up to play at Bobby Jones Golf Club. All had been caddies at the club, and one of the players, Robert Thomas, had contacted Thompson about playing there.

As reported in the *Herald*, Thompson advised Thomas that the city did not have the right to deny them playing.

To avoid any problems or misunderstanding that might ensue, Thompson notified the club manager, Harry Schaefer, that the foursome was coming.

There were no incidents, but the former hostess of the club, reflecting attitudes of days gone by, was quoted as saying, "When blacks tried to play there after World War II, I ran them off."

Karl Bickel wrote to Thompson that his "statesmanlike and far vision handling of the recent situation at the municipal golf club was so sound and so constructive that I'm moved to get to my typewriter and express my personal admiration and thanks."

Bickel felt that Thompson had forestalled what "could very easily have [become] an ugly situation on our hands...and be involved in one of those hopelessly stupid and dull tangles that are taking up so much of the municipal thinking about the South right now."

Recalling that day in a *Herald-Tribune* article twenty-five years later, Thomas said that blacks from as far away as Tampa would come to Sarasota to play, as it was the only course in the area where they were allowed. He thought it might have been the only course in the Southeast open to them.

In the same article, Thompson indicated that many municipalities sold their golf courses to private investors rather than integrate them, a decision they would later come to regret.

Former commissioner Jack Gurney told me that Thompson helped keep race relations "emotionally cooler here when other towns were going through turmoil. In his quiet, cerebral way, he helped Sarasota get through difficult times." In particular, Gurney cited that Thompson sought federal money to help put curbs, gutters and sidewalks in Newtown.

Former mayor Kerry Kirschner agreed. "The same thing wasn't happening in Bradenton," he said. He called Thompson a progressive in the area of race relations.

Barbara Thompson remembered how proud her husband was of the work being done in the Newtown area. He used to drive her around the area when they were putting the sidewalks down, pleased with the progress they made.

Some years later, Ed James, Sarasota civil rights leader and television personality, was quoted in a Bob Ardren article in the *Pelican Press*:

> *Ken Thompson and I had a real history—and it was a positive one. The community, especially the black community, will miss him because he was in office when big changes were happening across the country. He had the foresight and willingness to make the changes in Sarasota that benefitted us all, changes without all the turmoil that happened in other communities. I consider him a friend and will miss him.*

In recalling his early "activist-student days," Ed James, formerly a reporter for the *Sarasota Journal* and now into his fortieth year as the host on Channel 7's *Black Almanac*, recounted how he first came to know Ken Thompson.

He and two friends were back in town from Florida A&M University, and James announced it was about time to go to the "whites only" library in the Chidsey Library building on the North Trail and check out a book.

This was in 1957, and at the time if an African American wanted to check out a book, he would have to go to the Newtown Recreation Center and order the book to be sent from the Chidsey Library—a process that required two or three days.

James recalled that the three went into the library and were asked by the librarian what they were doing there. She informed them that if they wanted a book, they would have to follow the procedure and go to the Newtown Recreation Center. That was the policy; she did not make the rules, and she could not change them.

James, who did not know who Thompson was, told her they were not leaving and for her to call whoever she needed to get permission for them to check out a book. They fully expected to be arrested.

She called Thompson at city hall, and all James could hear was her saying to Thompson, "No. No. No." Finally, she turned the phone over to James.

Thompson introduced himself as the city manager and asked James who he was and what he wanted. After a brief conversation, he invited him and his friends to come to his office to discuss the situation further.

Fearing they were being set up to be arrested, one of the friends walked home instead, but James and Honor went to meet with Thompson.

Rebirth

Interior of the Chidsey Library Building, which was segregated until 1957, when a young Ed James, a Florida A&M student, decided to go there to check out a book. His request was refused. But after a meeting with Thompson, Thompson called the librarian and told her that from that time forward books could be checked out by anyone, regardless of race. *Sarasota County History Center.*

Thompson invited James and Honor into his office and questioned James about his background, asking who his parents and grandparents were. After a brief discussion, he agreed that they should be able to check out books from the city-run library.

Ed James had argued that his family paid taxes that supported the library, and he should have access to it.

Thompson agreed, picked up the phone, called the librarian and told her that, from that point on, the Chidsey Library would loan books regardless of race.

"That's how the Sarasota Library became integrated," said James.

James recalled that over the years, he and Thompson used the library episode as a personal code between them.

When community activist James sought help at city hall, meeting with city staff and Thompson to solve a problem or diffuse an issue, if Thompson told him, "Calm down, Ed, just remember the library," James knew he would

The Newtown Recreation Center was built in 1966 for $100,000 from the $4.1 million capital improvement bond money of 1964. Benjamin Steele was the architect for the project. Area resident and community activist Mrs. Elizabeth Seniors said the center was the most pressing need in Newtown. *Sarasota County History Center, Bill Blackstone Collection.*

get the help he sought. "If he said that, I could rest assured it was going to happen. He was always honest with me."

According to James, "Ken was a very positive influence in the community. He said what he meant and he meant what he said."

Years later, Thompson was criticized for not having any blacks as department heads. In a *Herald* article by Gregory Enns, Thompson defended himself: "The reason we have not got anybody up at that level is because

Rebirth

they're all capable of getting so much more money elsewhere. It isn't that we haven't been willing to do it."

He insisted that he was colorblind when it came to race.

Despite the promising growth, in April 1959, another attempt to oust Thompson was in the offing.

He came to expect occasional calls for his removal. In a Roy Porter interview for *Sarasota* magazine, he said, "About every five years or so there has been some movement toward taking away my job. You have to take it as probably a proper exercise of the political process."

He went on to note that differences between the manager and the commissioners were inherent in the system and attributed his longevity to being able to roll with the punches. "You can have a fundamental concept of what you want done, but those who are elected are representing the people, and they will decide."

Bickering at city hall had become so rampant that the term "cold war" was used to describe the atmosphere there.

On the one hand, Independent commissioners Mayor Frederick Dennis, Jack Turner and Herschel Hayo faced off against Frank Hoersting and Eddie Marable.

At a secret meeting held at the Lido Casino, the Independents choreographed the city manager's ouster. Hoersting and Marable were not invited and weren't even aware that the meeting was scheduled.

According to Sarasota historian John Ferrell, the Independents viewed Thompson as part of the old system and saw his ouster as the unfinished business that brought them to office. Ferrell indicated that Turner had asked Thompson to resign prior to the commission meeting. Thompson refused.

In explaining his actions, Turner said, "I promised the people when I campaigned for office that I would strive for a complete change in city government."

Hayo added that the ouster move had been under proposal since the December elections, when the Independents received a majority, which they took to be a mandate to sweep city hall. Thompson, they believed, had too much power.

At the city commission meeting on Monday, April 6, Turner put forth the resolution calling for Thompson to go. It was expected that Hayo would second that motion. But Hayo remained mute, and twice the motion died for lack of a second. Turner was obviously miffed. The meeting was adjourned until the next morning.

As rumors were rampant that a showdown regarding Thompson was in the offing, the Tuesday morning meeting in the commission chambers at the City Pier was filled to overflowing. Thompson supporters there included former commissioners Ben Hopkins, John Kicklighter, Ralph Farrell, A. Ray Howard, Jack O'Neill and John Binns.

A few of the commissioners remarked they had been barraged by citizens supporting Thompson, and at the commission meeting the crowd was overwhelmingly pro-Thompson and boisterous.

Farrell asked to be heard. He approached the edge of the commission table and demanded to know what the charges against Thompson were. "There has been a hassle all over town about this thing. Are you afraid... And will you not allow the public, who is vitally interested in this, to have anything to say on this resolution?" He was gaveled down by Dennis, who said, "The public is not invited at the commission meeting today. They're here as observers."

Commissioner Eddie Marable asked, "What terrible things has Thompson done?" and noted that in the three years he had been on the commission, he had always seen Thompson follow the commission policy.

Hayo, indicating that he had a continuous stream of pro-Thompson calls and visitors, said, "I learned many things I had not known before." He went on: "People seem to think that the City would be in dire straits without Thompson. If this situation of disaster without Thompson has truly been fostered and nurtured by the Commission, we as Commissioners should resign our authority to him."

Again, Marable asked, "What are these things that Thompson's done that we know nothing about?" He said to Turner, "I had the same phone calls... and without exception the people expressed concern over losing a good man who they think has done a good job."

Turner replied that it was his opinion that Thompson had not cooperated with the commission in carrying out policy.

Marable bristled, "This is my third year on the commission. I worked with Mr. Thompson, and it has been my observation in the past that regardless how he felt personally, when the commission laid down a rule, he carried it out to the best of his ability."

As to Turner's claim that Thompson had too much power, Hoersting indicated, "During the past year I served as mayor and worked with

Rebirth

Thompson in behalf of good government, and I will say he never once failed to carry out a commission policy to the best of his ability."

He continued, "We would be at a far less loss for the complete commission to resign than the City of Sarasota lose one of the best city managers that has ever come down the lane."

The *Herald* article described the audience reaction: "When the simple but powerful eloquence was over, bedlam broke loose. Cheers and shouts went up, and applause echoed through the chambers. The pulse of the people had been touched."

Turner said to Thompson, "I respect you as a man, and I have no hurt pride or feelings, nor do I think I could do a better job than you. I am acting in the interest of good government, and I am carrying out a promise I made when I was elected a year ago."

Through it all, Thompson was typically unruffled. He said not a word, watching the proceedings with an air of bemused detachment. The *Herald* reported, "Throughout it all Thompson had sat in cool, impassive silence. He seemed wrapped in a cloak [of] aloof dignity—with perhaps a trace of disdain."

Dennis, trying to gain control of the proceedings, reminded all that a motion had been put forward that required a second. After what must have seemed an eternity to Turner, neither Hayo nor anyone else seconded his motion. As the paper described the scene, "Dead, taut silence fell over the room. The seconds ticked away. Eyes darted about. The mayor fumbled with his gavel. Not a sound emerged from a throat."

Turner, "his face clouded with his distress," grabbed up his briefcase, swept his coat from the back of his chair and stared at Hayo. "I'd like to thank you, Mr. Hayo, very much," he said sarcastically and left the room.

The meeting ended with more cheers from the crowd. Before he left the chambers, Thompson said simply, "I'm glad to continue to serve the city commission and the people of Sarasota to the best of my ability."

Earlier, he had said if the entire commission did not want his services, he would resign, but he would not be forced out on a three-two vote.

Turner called a press conference for that afternoon to explain his actions, stating that he "acted in good faith" and reiterating his belief that Thompson had not followed commission policy "in the manner we so desired." He gave no specifics.

The resolution that was not read for want of a second stated:

> *The City Commission deems it for the best interests of the City of Sarasota that the employment of the incumbent City Manager, Kenneth Thompson,*

be immediately terminated. Such removal shall be effective immediately upon adoption of this resolution unless otherwise provided by law.

A Western Union telegram in the Thompson papers from Sarasota resident Alton M. Heistad spoke for many: "Congratulations Mr. Thompson, the real honest people of this city are with you heart and soul."

4

SARASOTA GOES MODERN AND OUTWARD

The 1960s

Elected officials set policies and the manager carries them out.
—*Ken Thompson*

While the city was marching forward, so too was the county picking up its share of newcomers. The countywide population of Sarasota in 1950 was 28,827, with 18,896 living within the city limits and the remaining 9,931 spread throughout the rest of the county.

By 1960, the city's population was 34,083, while the county increased to 42,812, and the outward spread was hurting downtown Sarasota, heretofore the heart of the community.

Mom and pop businesses were losing customers to Ringling and Southgate shopping centers, theatergoers were buying tickets at the new movie houses and downtown hotels were hurting for guests who seemed to prefer the beaches for lodging.

And instead of driving along Highway U.S. 41 on Main Street, out-of-towners—prospective customers—were bypassing the downtown core on the new four-lane highway.

The only real good news for downtown was the addition of Maas Brothers Department Store, which opened to the public on October 1, 1956. Ten thousand people were on hand for the grand opening of the store, which was managed for many years by John Schaub Jr. The store sold everything from outboard motors, garden supplies and swing sets, as well as appliances,

Thompson in 1961, when he was appointed to the League of Municipalities. *Courtesy Barbara Thompson.*

Sarasota Goes Modern and Outward

jewelry and clothing. But as it was located at Main Street and Washington Boulevard, it was really too far from the central hub to do much good for most of the downtown merchants.

———◆———

Sarasota, known throughout the world as the Circus City, was soon to lose the Ringling Bros. and Barnum & Bailey Circus to Venice.

Ever since December 1927, when John Ringling brought the circus to town to bolster the faltering economy and draw more tourists, the headquarters had been a major attraction, and trappings of the

John Ringling brought the Winter Headquarters of the Ringling Bros. & Barnum and Bailey to Sarasota from Bridgeport, Connecticut, in 1927 to help bolster the local economy. It became the biggest tourist attraction in the state until Disney World opened in Orlando. The Greatest Show on Earth moved to Venice in 1960. Wherever the circus traveled, Sarasota, the Circus City, was advertised in its brochures and on its billboards. *Sarasota County History Center.*

circus were seen throughout the community: backyard riggings of the aerialists, Circus Day sales, circus themes in restaurants and live circus performances, circus benefits for St. Martha's Church, circus parades associated with the annual Sara de Sota Pageant and the Circus Hall of Fame. Schoolmates were often circus performers, and the Ringling name seemed to be everywhere. Even one of the telephone exchanges was RIngling.

But by the end of the 1950s, the circus scene seemed to belong to a different place in time. The *Herald* noted an undercurrent of bad feeling engendered by the circus bosses. "They have been all out to get everything possible for the circus...After realizing about $350,000 profit on the sale (of land that had been obtained from the county without cost), the circus officials asked for more free land for the new operation. But the time for the free ride had ended."

The *Herald* wished the circus well in Venice and assured readers that "Sarasota had enough tourist attractions to complement the sun and sand and would continue to draw tourists from the world over."

In 1960, the circus left Sarasota, and today the Glen Oaks Subdivision is on the former site of the circus Winter Quarters.

With the newly completed highway along the downtown bay front, and the completion of the new Ringling Causeway, the next move to modernize that area of the city was the creation of Island Park and a new marina, to replace the aging and antiquated buildings on the city pier and increase the number of boat slips.

Island Park, a rabbit leg–shaped peninsula, was to be an eleven-acre, multipurpose breakwater for the marina. The dredging was finished in

Opposite, top: Looking east from Sarasota Bay toward Five Points, 1958. The white area is the dredge upon which U.S. 41 would be rerouted along the bay front. Downtown, the three tall buildings are the Orange Blossom Hotel to the right, the Hotel Sarasota to the left and, at Five Points, the Palmer Bank. *Sarasota County History Center, Pete Esthus Collection.*

Opposite, bottom: Construction underway on Marina Mar; the complex was designed by architect Robert L. Shaw and built by E.E. "Gene" Simmons to put Sarasota on the yachtsman's map. *Sarasota County History Center, Pete Esthus Collection.*

Sarasota Goes Modern and Outward

City Planner R.W. "Bob" Pavitt, always a busy man at city hall, looking over some plans. Pavitt, a former aviator in the Pacific during World War II, was head of planning in Sarasota from 1955 to 1966 and then moved to Juneau, Alaska. *Sarasota County History Center.*

February 1964, and the bulk heading was completed shortly thereafter. Erwin Gremli II was chosen as the architect for the Island Park Building, expected to cost $25,000, with Thompson recommending, and the commission agreeing, that the city should bear the full cost of the building so that it could exercise total control over it.

The need for a new first-class marina was high on the list of items sought by the city. In 1963, the commission approved plans for $300,000 for dredging and bulk heading, with private capital to help fund the marina.

Sarasota Goes Modern and Outward

Rendering of Marina Mar on Sarasota Bay. After the company went broke, Jack Graham took over the business and ran it as Marina Jack. *Sarasota County History Center.*

Named Marina Mar, the project would have 143 boat slips, fueling facilities for boats, an upscale restaurant, shops, a snack bar and amenities for the boaters. It was intended to put Sarasota on the yachtsman's map.

Thompson was aware of the snob appeal effect the marina would have on the wealthy. He noted in the *Herald*, "Prospective customers could look down from their windows, and you could show them where they could keep their boats, their yachts."

John O. Binns, the former mayor who had pushed for the project, said, "I think this is one of the greatest days in Sarasota's modern history. The birth of the baby was very, very painful, but I think it was good. Sarasota is back on the road of high quality development."

The Marina Mar complex was designed by architect Robert L. Shaw and built by E.E. "Gene" Simmons.

The city and Marina Mar, Inc., signed a thirty-year lease, allowing Mira Mar the right to build and operate the marina. It called for an initial expenditure of $250,000 within one year. On hand with city officials for the signing was the always-busy city planning director, R.W. Pavitt.

Marina Mar, Inc., soon failed—twice in fact—and was taken over by businessman Jack Graham, from Effingham, Illinois, who owned a Plymouth, Chrysler, Imperial dealership there and three Holiday Inns. He transformed Marina Mar into Marina Jack and guided it as it grew with the community. He called the area "Sarasota's front porch" and ran it for over thirty-three years.

The dredging and paving along the bay front without landscaping made for a stark scene until the area was landscaped. When it was finally beautified, Garden Club president Mrs. Gladys Morton wrote a letter to the commission "highly approving the projects on the North Trail, Harding Circle, along the Ringling Causeway and the bay front, and the Island Park Marina."

An aerial photograph of Sarasota's downtown in 1964, looking west from Palm Avenue, illustrated how much the old Sarasota was being overshadowed by the new.

In the forefront of the photo were the '20s boom-era buildings showing their age: Mira Mar Apartments and Mira Mar Hotel, Orange Blossom Hotel, Hotel Sarasota and small businesses along Main Street.

At Gulfstream Avenue and west were the new Gulf Stream Towers and the old city hall building, surrounded by the rerouted Highway U.S. 41, Island Park and the preparatory work for Marina Mar.

The ten-story Gulf Stream Towers, the first major high-rise building on Gulfstream Avenue, was designed by noted Sarasota School of Architecture architect Edward J. "Tim" Seibert. The building was expected to cost $1,700,000, and Seibert said, "The apartments are

Opposite, top: It's 1965, and Island Park is in the process of being landscaped. Marina Mar, which later failed, was taken over by Jack Graham, who called it Marina Jack and ran it for thirty-three years. He called this area "Sarasota's front porch." *Sarasota County History Center, Pete Esthus Collection.*

Opposite, bottom: Looking west toward Sarasota Bay. The white building is the Gulf Stream Towers, "Sarasota's Prestige Address," designed by noted and prolific architect Tim Seibert of the Sarasota School of Architecture. Golden Gate Point is to the right, and Island Park is to the left. *Sarasota County History Center.*

Sarasota Goes Modern and Outward

The Rise of Sarasota

"A Tradition of Inspired Living" awaits at Plymouth Harbor on Coon Key. At twenty-five stories, it is still one of the largest buildings in Sarasota. Designed by architects Frank Folsom Smith and Louis F. Schneider, according to Plymouth Harbor's website, Smith's inspiration for the building was the Brown Palace Hotel, a Denver landmark. The luxury retirement center has 210 independent living residences. *Sarasota County History Center.*

designed on the motif of the fashionable apartments that have made up the bay front of Rio de Janeiro."

Seibert was one of the most prolific of this group of architects who were gaining critical and international acclaim for their work here, while casting the international spotlight on modern Sarasota.

They were helping to refashion the look of Sarasota. Mentored to a great extent by Board of Public Instruction chairman Philip Hiss, they were responsible for a number of innovative school designs, including Victor Lundy's Alta-Vista with its "butterfly wing," the renowned Paul Rudolph's Riverview High School, a new addition to Sarasota High School, Ralph and William Zimmerman's Brookside Junior High School, the Summerhouse Restaurant of Carl Abbott, Seibert's Siesta Key Pavilion, Jack West's

Sarasota Goes Modern and Outward

Nokomis Beach Pavilion and Frank Folsom Smith's Plymouth Harbor on Coon Key, at twenty-five stories the tallest building in Sarasota.

Homes and buildings of these architects were often featured in regional, national and international magazines, garnering great publicity for Sarasota. Plymouth Harbor was described as one of the most beautiful locations in America in *Florida Architect* magazine.

Thompson was a big fan of their work and often recommended them for city projects. His own home in Harbor Acres had been designed by William Zimmerman.

Infrastructure needs required a major boost, and in 1964 a bond issue in the amount of $4.1 million and touted by the city as "Paths to Progress" would supply the stimulus needed to move forward.

Stumping for a favorable vote, Thompson, who did not usually make speeches, spoke to the Rotary Club, calling the bond "vitally necessary to preserve Sarasota's image as a city of refinement and culture—a city of progressive, alert ideas so it will not sink into economic ignominy."

As the date for the vote drew nearer, he warned, "Sarasota must begin to prepare for its role in the future when large cities will continue to grow and small cities will remain stationary or decline."

The Sarasota County Civic League agreed, noting that the bond issue must be approved "if Sarasota is to regain its now tarnished image as a community of culture and equality, not to mention our lagging economy."

The bond contained eight separate components, which were to be voted on individually: $750,000 for a new city hall; $150,000 for city shops; $1,350,000 for a new civic theater; $100,000 for a Newtown Recreation Center; $100,000 for sidewalks to schools; $1,100,000 for a planned east–west traffic loop; $300,000 for Lido Beach improvement; and $250,000 to modernize the Lido Casino.

It was estimated that it would cost each taxpayer a penny a day, and on the election day, December 8, 1964, the *Herald* editorialized in favor of passage of all eight components: "Each represents an investment in a healthy future for a city that ought to go first class. Approval...will be an affirmation that this is the direction Sarasota wants to take."

The measure passed by more than two to one.

The only commission race that year went to Jack Betz, who unseated Herschel Hayo.

The Rise of Sarasota

Sarasota was desperately in need of a new facility to conduct the city's business and had been for quite a long time.

The old Hover Arcade on Sarasota Bay, a Neoclassical tan brick building with an inviting archway onto the pier, had served the city since 1917, when it was purchased for $39,581.34 from the Hover brothers, Dr. William, Frank B. and J.O., winter residents of Lima, Ohio.

The brothers had purchased the dock from mayor, councilman and Siesta Key developer Harry Higel in 1911 and began making improvements. The arcade was built in 1913.

The building became a symbol of Sarasota—the logo on city government and chamber of commerce stationery.

For a time, the chamber of commerce had an office there, and another tenant, J.C. Cash, whose son Joe was a world champion water skier in the 1950s, offered skiing lessons. During World War II, the Enlisted Men's Service Club was in one of the old buildings.

Some city staffers recalled lazy summer days when they could drop a fishing line into the water from their office windows—presumably when Thompson was not around.

As Sarasota blossomed after World War II, the Hover Arcade had outlived its usefulness. It was woefully inadequate to conduct the business of a modern city. A picture of the building on a pamphlet explaining the 1964 bond referendum had OBSOLETE stamped across it, and it was demolished in September 1967.

According to Stan Zimmerman, longtime newspaper reporter, author and avid sailor, after World War II, the Sailing Squadron had been meeting at the Hover Arcade on the old pier.

Zimmerman, who covered Thompson for WSPB radio and WXLT television from 1975 to 1978 and 1983 to 1986, said "he was a patient teacher of commissioners and reporters alike. Getting stuff right was a passion with him."

Zimmerman recalled that when the building was razed, "Ken offered the sailors a barren plot of land on City Island. The sailors snapped it up, and signed a 'perpetual' lease with the city for $1/year." (After 1986, the city began charging the Squadron.)

Zimmerman indicated, "In many respects, Ken is the principal founder of the Sarasota Sailing Squadron, which many perceive as one of the few remaining 'old Sarasota' places still around."

Sarasota Goes Modern and Outward

Sarasota's prolific architect Jack West, a talented member of the Sarasota School of Architecture, drew the plans for the new city hall. As he recalled the assignment in his book *The Lives of An Architect*, "A $1,000,000 budget was whittled down to $600,000, and the low bid, put in by local contractor Gene Simmons was $840,000. The budget would not be increased and the building size could not be reduced." As West put it, "The architect could not eat or sleep."

Although West indicated that the finished product was a "far cry" from his initial plans, it still retained some of his original concepts. Of the signature Jack Cartlidge sculpture *Nobody's Listening*, he indicated that Mr. Cartlidge "produced a $100,000 monumental sculpture in copper for $4,000."

The Jack West-designed city hall on First Street was ready for occupancy in 1967. Former mayor Lou Ann Palmer told me that Thompson had West put audience seats in the chambers above the city commissioners so that the commissioners would have to look up at the citizens, who were their bosses, not the other way around. *Sarasota County History Center.*

West wrote, "Within one year after completion a city commissioner fell into one of the pools and ordered the pools in the east–west walkway filled with concrete."

The new city hall was dedicated on December 12, 1967, and seventeen former mayors and city commissioners attended. Mayor Betz intoned of the city's previous leaders, "The image of this building was dreamed of for years by these gentlemen."

Five-term mayor Lou Ann Palmer gave insight into the democratic mind of Thompson. She said he believed the people were the boss, not the city commissioners, and he told West that he wanted the commission chambers designed so that the citizens would be above the commissioners, accounting for the amphitheater we have today. The commissioners would have to look up at the citizens, not the other way around.

And he did not want the public to stand uncomfortably in front of the commissioners at a dais when they spoke. He had West place seating directly in front of the commission table, so that those having to speak to the commissioners would be eye to eye as equals when they discussed city business.

To Thompson, the people, the voters, were paramount, not the commissioners.

In 1968, the design of city hall won an award from the Florida Association of the American Institute of Architects, which cited it as "a place to carry on municipal business without pomposity," an accolade appreciated by Ken Thompson.

In October 1966, Thompson had a déjà vu experience.

The commission that year was made up of Mayor David Cohen and Commissioners Jack Betz, Gil Waters, Glenn Rose and William Montgomery.

Writing for the *Herald*, Bill Zellmer headlined his story "Power Struggle or Family Squabble?" and wrote that while Cohen and Rose stood "solidly behind the City Manager and Betz, promising, 'Under no circumstances would I like to see the City Manager leave,' Waters and Montgomery were unhappy with Thompson's performance." Waters was quoted as saying, "You can't blame someone for not being totally perfect, but you can criticize for not making an effort to follow directives."

Years later, Waters was quoted in the *Florida Accent* as saying that Thompson's conservatism had left the city with "a negative action program about quality growth. And what we've had is growth that has come in spite of that attitude and that is not always the best way."

The squabble lacked the fireworks of the 1953 and 1959 showdowns, and Thompson, who never argued his point in the press, was typically silent.

Betz noted that if Thompson was setting policy, "The commission is letting him do it. If he is doing it, it is the fault or weakness of this city commission."

Rose and Cohen saw no examples of Thompson setting policy, and former commissioners spoke in favor of Thompson and the manner in which he conducted city business.

Former commissioner Robert Anson said, "You can look all over the country, but I don't think you'll be able to find a better man for Sarasota as far as the citizens and taxpayers are concerned. You can build all sorts of palaces above the ground but unless you have things like adequate water supplies and storm sewers, what will it mean?"

Former mayor Herschel Hayo, a firm Thompson supporter, said that he did not recall anyone running on the platform of firing Thompson. He was of the opinion that if someone ran, trumpeting the removal of the city manager, that person would "be soundly beaten."

He added that "after seven years of service to Sarasota and many years of being on the outside and looking in, I'm mighty pleased with the services of Ken Thompson."

About Thompson's long tenure, former mayor Overton was quoted as saying, "He never flaps. He has self-confidence. He has survived many commissions. His attitude is I was here when they came and I'll be here when they're gone."

Thompson soldiered on. In December 1966, he was honored by being chosen to be the president of the Florida League of Municipalities, an organization that numbered 331 member cities out of a total 385 cities in Florida.

It was a prestigious honor. In accepting the position, he issued a statement in the *Florida Municipal Record*. Noting the problems being faced by quickly growing cities, he wrote that care should be taken to ensure the intrinsic beauty of Florida cities: "Let me suggest that in our striving for municipal order we should not neglect civic beauty, for sterile orderliness is not sufficient in itself. Florida cities have always been noted for their beauty and urban proliferation should not be permitted to emasculate this quality."

In 1966, the $3.75 million Verna Well Field project was completed. Located seventeen miles northeast of Sarasota on 1,800 acres, the water from the field would help supply the needs of Sarasota's increasing population. It was reported that initially 10 million gallons of water could be pumped daily and that number could be boosted to 20 million gallons with the construction of a booster station.

The year 1966 was also when Sarasota loaned Thompson a city-use Pontiac Catalina—a four-door behemoth capable of carrying one city manager/driver and five city commissioners/passengers to and from meetings.

In those casual days before Government in the Sunshine laws were passed, the car was a rolling commission chambers, where agendas and issues were often hacked out and differences resolved ahead of the city commission meeting at city hall. The drives to the Lido Casino or the Bobby Jones Golf Course to discuss city business ahead of the evening commission meeting became legendary.

The Pontiac was a white four-door model and cost the city $2,711.98. Thompson expressly asked for no power steering so that he could exercise his shoulders while maneuvering it but requested that it come equipped with air conditioning. He kept the car for so long that Mrs. Thompson joked it was the oldest car in Sarasota—by far the oldest vehicle in the city fleet. He did not have an assigned parking space. He parked it wherever he could near city hall and walked to work.

After Thompson drove it for twenty-one years, he turned it back over to the city. Eventually, the car, which had been repainted, was auctioned for $200.00, thus ending up costing the city $119.61 a year, a number with which Thompson could live.

Former mayor Elmer Berkel said, "Thompson had made the car a symbol, an example to other city employees. He would not get a new car but would continue to use it as long as it was serviceable."

While there was no talk of renovating the old Hover Arcade, the bond issue of 1964 provided for the remodeling of the Lido Casino, Sarasota's glorious beachfront hallmark since 1940, which had been deteriorating badly.

The casino was another of the major Works Progress Administration projects that helped Sarasota make it through the Great Depression.

As Sarasota's financial well-being was closely linked to the annual migratory habits of the "snowbirds," in 1936, the Chamber of Commerce Committee to Create Summer Business met to determine what could be done to boost summer business, the slowest time of the year.

It was longtime real estate man and publisher of the *Sarasota Visitors Guide* Roger Flory who suggested that the city provide a municipal bathing beach. The next year, that idea was expanded to include a bathing facility.

Sarasota Goes Modern and Outward

The lovely Sarasota Sun Debs posing at the Lido Casino Pool on Lido Beach. Opening to wide acclaim in 1940, this was one of Sarasota's most popular recreation and social gathering venues to dance, dine, drink, sunbathe, swim, hold political rallies, attend sporting events and just people watch. It was razed in 1969 and is missed to this day. *Sarasota County History Center, Bill Blackstone Collection.*

Karl A. Bickel was appointed to chair a committee to take the matter up with the city council, and thus was sown the seed that would ultimately blossom into the Lido Casino.

The site deemed the most desirable for the project was a 1,300-foot stretch of Lido Beach owned by the estate of John Ringling, then under the control of Ringling's nephew and co-executor of his estate, John Ringling North.

Mayor Verman Kimbrough met with North, and an agreement was reached whereby the property would be deeded to the city in exchange for $35,000, which sum would immediately be paid back to the city for delinquent taxes.

Albert Moore Saxe drew up preliminary plans for a "Hawaiian-style" casino called Sarasands.

Ralph Twitchell, one of the founders of the Sarasota School of Architecture, was given the assignment, and his version of the Lido Casino was one of Sarasota's first modern buildings. Sarasota, according to the *Herald*, "should be very happy."

From the time of its conception, progress on the casino was front-page news, where it often competed for space with ominous headlines from Europe, which was sliding into World War II.

It was hoped that construction would be completed by the summer of 1939. A color rendering appeared on the cover of that year's edition of *Flory's Visitors Guide* with the description: "Whether it's fun and frolic…recreation or amusement…health and happiness…or just plain lazy contentment. The Sarasota Lido beckons all who seek what Florida has most to give."

The casino was opened to the public on May 23, 1940, and thousands swarmed to what was by then being touted as the "$250,000 Lido Beach Municipal Casino." A page of photos in the *Herald* showed the throngs at play—diving off the high board, enjoying the view from the second-floor terrace, children splashing in the circular wading pool—quite a contrast from the glum Depression and European war news.

The casino also featured two dining rooms, the Castaways Bar, a ballroom, a grill, a dressing pavilion, beach cabanas and a freshwater pool where future city commissioner and mayor Jack Betz lifeguarded.

When World War II started, the casino was the number one place for service personnel training at the Sarasota Army Air Base to go on leave. Most of the trainees had never before been away from home, and it is not difficult to imagine the visual impact of the casino. It was like nothing they, or the locals, for that matter, had ever seen—a vision of tropical splendor—and the soldiers would take memories of the casino wherever they went.

It was also the "in place" for any number of events: political rallies, proms, dining, drinking, dancing to the music of Rudy Bundy, card parties, people watching, swimming and gymnastic events. There seemed to be something for everyone.

In 1955, the casino, still billed as one of the major attractions on the West Coast of Florida, was beginning to show signs of wear from the salt air, the sea, the sun and untold thousands of visitors. It was looking older than its years.

At the same time, Lido Key was enjoying a building spree of fine homes, modern hotels and resorts: Surf & Sand, the Azure Tides with its Viking Room restaurant for fine dining, the seven-story Three Crowns, the Triton Hotel, the Sandcastle, Lido Biltmore and others.

The appearance of the area was taking on an upscale look, and the casino was not keeping up. In an article for *The News*, A.J. Ruttenber reported,

Sarasota Goes Modern and Outward

The USS *Sarasota*, the county's namesake ship, served in World War II and was reactivated to fight in the Korean War. In 1951 and 1952, the ship made a visit to Sarasota, anchored two miles offshore and staged a mock invasion of Lido Beach. Nearly nine thousand people turned out for the event and were ferried back and forth to the ship for guided tours. For three days, the community rolled out the red carpet for the 50 officers and 450 crew men. *Sarasota County History Center, Bill Blackstone Collection.*

"The Casino is not quite up to the plush atmosphere which is beginning to penetrate Lido." He wrote that it was giving the city a headache. It was also competing with the area hospitality businesses, drawing away customers.

In March 1959, when the city commission voted to advertise for proposals to lease the casino's operations, an angry Commissioner Hayo said, "This thing is outrageous—it is mismanagement."

The casino had not been a big moneymaker since the war. And the temporary removal of the liquor operation in 1958 further decreased revenue and trimmed the number of visitors.

The 1960 budget allocated $30,000 for general cleanup and repair, with more promised for 1961. With the $250,000 from the 1964 bond, the hope was that the casino could be brought back to its former inviting condition.

The Rise of Sarasota

It was not. The casino was demolished in February 1969. The general consensus seems to be that it went down because of Ken Thompson. Only one commissioner, Jack Betz, voted not to demolish it.

Some years ago, when this writer asked Thompson why the casino was not saved, I found it telling that he did not reply, "Ask the commissioners who voted to demolish it." He could have said, "I just made a recommendation." But he knew the importance of his input in the decision, and he would not pass the buck.

He was tired of dealing with the myriad headaches and costs that came with the casino, so he took responsibility for its destruction, responsibility that he could have rightfully shared with the commission.

He told me that, the bond issue of 1964 notwithstanding, the people "voted" by not using the facility as they had in the past. "The allure was gone," he said. "Whereas the city had once recognized the need for the Lido Casino as a tourist inducement, it had outlived its usefulness in that regard. People are more likely to go to a facility in the park, which is what we have today."

The numbers would seem to bear him out. For the fiscal year 1957–58, $12,850 was generated from cabana rentals. From 1966 to 1967, that number fell to just $2,576.

For Thompson, the Lido Casino may have been the crown jewel of yesterday's Sarasota, now tarnished and a constant pull on the municipal purse. In any case, its Seibert-designed replacement, while lacking the glamour, was more cost efficient and has lasted to this day.

When the "minicasino" was completed, Commissioners Tony Saprito and David Cohen, along with Thompson, Seibert and a few other city officials, took a tour. Seibert indicated that the word casino was no longer appropriate as the new structure did not have a large room.

After the tour, the group said they liked what they saw. Only the pool remained.

At the time of the casino's razing, the beach on which it stood was eroding badly. The city owned all the property north of the casino to the pass, while everything south was privately owned.

The Army Corps of Engineers was expected to undertake the renourishing job, but because easements could not be obtained from the motel and hotel owners along the way, the corps could not participate.

Thompson, who was an expert in the science of beach preservation and a founding member of the Florida Shore and Beach Preservation Association, wanted to proceed without them.

Don Smally indicated, "City Manager Ken Thompson recommended to the city commission that the city proceed alone. The city authorized Smally Wellford & Nalven to do the engineering for a project on city-owned land only."

Ultimately, the Ardaman & Associates of Orlando pumped 600,000 cubic yards of sand on the beach. And while the sand was not as fine as it had been previously, Smally said it was the best they could get from where they had to dredge.

5

REGROUPING

The 1970s

He was the greatest. There'll never be another one like him.
—*Mayor Fred Soto*

For Thompson, the hallmark building of the new Sarasota was the Lewis and Eugenia Van Wezel Performing Arts Hall.

Ground was broken on the hall on April 25, 1968, and a photo appeared in the *Herald* showing Commissioner David Cohen; Mayor Jack Betz; Thompson; Adolph "Chick" Frankel, chairman of the auditorium advisory committee; and Paul Stannard, who had helped obtain a $430,000 grant from the Van Wezel Foundation. Each had a shovel to push into the turf.

Betz credited David Cohen "as the man who conceived the building." He went on, "This is a great day for Sarasota and citizens of the county and other surrounding areas. This building exemplifies the character of the citizens and of the community perhaps more than any other structure."

Cohen was a musician, a child prodigy violinist who was a co-founder of the Florida West Coast Symphony and, in its early years, its business manager, president and concertmaster. To him the need for a new hall was acute, and he spearheaded the effort to build the Van Wezel.

When Cohen died in 1999, Dr. Curtis Haug, the hall's managing director, said, "It will always be a monument to his total commitment to all areas of Sarasota's cultural life."

Indeed, it was a giant step forward for the cultural life of Sarasota. Previously, live entertainment was served up in the Mira Mar Auditorium, the Mediterranean Revival–designed hall on McAnsh Square that had been built in 1924, its opening called the "Event of the Season"

It was not the venue to entice top-flight talent. Jazz dance bands passing through town played there, as did soprano Josephine Lucchese, an understudy to Helen Morgan. Baritone Robert Ringling, Charles Ringling's son, a noted opera singer, put on a concert, as did Frieda Hempel, the "Jenny Lind of Today." Lowell Thomas lectured to a full house, with "Lawrence in Arabia and Allenby in Palestine."

It was also used for numerous community events, from flower shows to fashion shows. But by 1955, its best years were behind it, and it was demolished.

The other major entertainment venue, the cavernous Works Progress Administration–funded Municipal Auditorium, hosted and continues to host various events. It was built without regard to acoustics—an unrefined workhorse of a building that was opened in time for the annual Sara de Sota Pageant on February 24, 1938, and serves a multitude of civic functions: proms, dances, beauty pageants, home shows, flea markets, flower shows, and various performances.

Neither lent themselves to the high caliber of entertainment that modern Sarasota sought, but the Lewis and Eugenia Van Wezel Performing Arts Hall would bring world-class productions and talent.

Progress on the construction of the unusual-looking but beautiful building on Sarasota Bay was closely followed, derided by some as the "Purple People Seater" or "Purple Cow."

Designed by the renowned William Wesley Peters of Taliesin, of the Frank Lloyd Wright Foundation, the color scheme, floor coverings and fabrics were selected by Mrs. Frank Lloyd Wright, and the project director, Vernon D. Swaback, predicted that over time "people will understand it and with more exposure be as enthusiastic as we are." He declared, "The purple color may have a harsh appearance now but it will fade to smoother lavender with a little time."

Opposite, top: The cavernous Municipal Auditorium was better for car shows than concerts. What Sarasota desperately needed was a new concert hall, for which Mayor Cohen pushed hard along with Ken Thompson, who saw Sarasota's success tied closely to its cultural offerings. *Sarasota County History Center, Bill Blackstone Collection.*

Opposite, bottom: Mayor Cohen, the driving force in making the Van Wezel Hall a reality, with Thompson, 1977. *Barney Stein Photographer, courtesy Barbara Thompson.*

Regrouping

Thompson with architect Vernon Swaback displaying a flag designed by the Frank Lloyd Wright Foundation's Department of Graphics and Heraldry. As reported in the *Sarasota Herald*, the flag at left shows the city logo on a central band of earth green bordered by two blue bands representing the sky and sea. At right is the Performing Arts Hall banner, an interlocking geometric shape symbolic of the arts hall–community interrelationship. *Courtesy Barbara Thompson.*

When the controversial color was decided, Swaback sent a letter to William C. Coleman, chairman of the Van Wezel Hall's operating committee: "In summary, we can only ask for a reasonable amount of faith in our professional judgment and the record it has produced."

The hall was said to cost $2,475,000, and Peters, discussing the building some years later with *Herald* writer Charlie Huisking, said, "The design was suggested by a serrated, lavender colored seashell that had come in my possession. It was designed to reflect its waterfront location and the entire West Coast of Florida environment."

He told Huisking, "I had shown the shell to Mrs. Frank Lloyd Wright and she said, 'Why not paint it the same color as the shell?'"

Thompson had remarked of the local controversy engendered by the hall, "If a building doesn't provoke some kind of discussion then it probably isn't a successful piece of architecture."

Regrouping

St. Pete Times Art and Architecture writer Charles Benbow assured doubters that Sarasota could be proud of it. As it was designed by "one of the world's most famous architectural groups," that alone "will guarantee wide recognition for the hall...and draw sightseers off highway U.S. 41 for many years."

At its completion, county commissioner William Carey congratulated the city on its achievement.

"It's magnificent, really magnificent," he said. "It's the most outstanding civic accomplishment to date. It will do much to improve and stabilize the cultural image of Sarasota."

Its opening on January 5, 1970, was a suitably grand affair, and it was given high marks by attendees on hand to watch the performance of *The Fiddler on the Roof*. All agreed that Sarasota, the cultural capital of the Gulf Coast, finally had a first-class venue to book top-drawer productions and artists. This was a symbol of modern Sarasota—beautiful, refined and cultured.

On the day the floor was installed at the Van Wezel Performing Arts Hall, Thompson and Barbara were called over for a champagne toast, with Thompson joking that his juggling was the first act in the new hall. *Courtesy Barbara Thompson.*

On opening night, Mayor Overton addressed the audience for a few minutes before the curtain went up, saying, "I know all of you will join me in saluting the latest gem in the Bayfront Tiara of the city of Sarasota. We all must surely admit that our new gem is an amethyst."

He read a congratulatory telegram from Governor Claude R. Kirk: "It is another outstanding example of why Florida living is the very finest."

Audience reaction on that opening night was favorable. Dick Bloom of the *Herald* wrote: "Comments made by first-nighters as they entered the richly endowed grand foyer of the theatre included the repeated use of such equally splendorous adjectives as 'magnificent,' 'tremendous,' 'awesome,' and more to exhaust the most complete of dictionaries."

For effect, William Wesley Peters arrived dressed in a purple tuxedo.

No one had followed the progress of the construction more closely than Thompson. When Peters was in town, he often stayed at the Thompson residence, and when the floor to the hall stage was put in, Vernon Swaback, one of the architects, and Ken and Barbara Thompson went over to have a celebratory glass of champagne, with Thompson doing a juggling act, kidding that he was the first to perform at the hall.

So close had the Thompsons and Peters become that when Peters was married to Svetlana Alliluyeva, Mrs. Frank Lloyd Wright invited them to a reception in their honor at Taliesin West, in Scottsdale, Arizona.

Less than a month after the Van Wezel Hall opened, Thompson celebrated his twentieth anniversary as city manager of Sarasota. He was nearly sixty years old. His hair was graying, his eyes still a vivid blue. He was in great shape mentally and physically—as always, a presence to reckon with.

Downtown was filling in with high-rise condominiums and multistoried office buildings that housed banks, law offices and other professions.

It had sometimes been a rocky ride, but through it all, Thompson had remained calm in the face of adversity and gracious in accepting community acclaim for his accomplishments. He never bragged and always shared credit with the commission he served and the staff he worked with. "Many unseen hands work with you," he said, adding, "A city manager is prone to get too much credit for progress."

In an interview with Lee Butcher of the *Herald*, who noted his rather sparse office—no degrees, honors or plaques on the walls—Thompson said,

Regrouping

"I threw away the trappings a long time ago. I don't have much use for them. They're trappings of ignorance."

Only a few paintings of his daughter, Laura, adorned the walls.

Butcher remarked, "Thompson was a man who is confident in his own ability without being offensive about it."

Twenty years on the job in Sarasota, four times longer than the average stay of a city manager, Thompson summed up his philosophy of the position: "This job is a service to the public."

He told Butcher that over the years he had observed a trend toward pluralism in decision-making. "The individual cannot make a unilateral decision anymore. Several people are involved. This has led to city managers around the country becoming diplomats."

Perhaps recalling disagreements with the commission, he said, "We don't always think the same way. If we did, something would be wrong. You have to have different thoughts about things in order to have progress."

At a city commission meeting, to mark his twentieth anniversary, Thompson was given a sheet cake with a single candle. The cake was decorated to represent Sarasota Bay with a sailboat regatta. As he blew out the candle, his remark, "This is the first day of the next twenty years," was almost right on the mark.

Waldo Proffitt, managing editor of the Lindsay Newspapers, which included the *Sarasota Herald* and the *Sarasota Journal*, knew Thompson well. He believed Thompson had a vision for Sarasota's future. "He did not hesitate to share his view with commissioners, usually one-on-one. He did not go around town making speeches or talking to reporters about what the city should do, but if commissioners asked in public for his advice, he gave it in public logically and unemotionally."

Judge John Scheb, who had been the city attorney for eleven years, agreed. "Ken had the vision to always see the long-range consequences of any significant municipal action."

One of the few times Thompson aired his differences with the commission in the press occurred in March 1973, when the commission passed a resolution supporting a local service club's wish to sell advertising on park benches to raise money for one of its projects. Thompson did not contain himself.

Herald reporter Len Antell reported that he exclaimed, "I'm exorcised, I've never been so upset over anything. This town of all places should not permit advertising on benches."

Selling advertisement space did not fit in with the city manager's vision of Sarasota. It was an unnecessary, albeit minor, blemish.

He said of the commission rationale that one of the commissioners was a member of the club that wanted the advertising, another felt it was a good way to provide people with benches and the third commissioner, well, who knew what was on his mind?

Thompson came under fire in the community for his utterances and was defended by Proffitt, who said the abuse he was receiving was undeserved, reminding everyone that "Ken Thompson has been very good for Sarasota. And [still] is."

On May 13, 1973, Thompson was tapped for the cover story of the *Tampa Tribune*'s Florida Accent Sunday supplement. Titled "The Charmed Life of Ken Thompson," it provided a comprehensive account of his tenure as the long-serving city manager.

The Jim Toner article reported that Thompson had "staged one of the longest-running municipal shows in the nation, aided by a good sense of timing and knowing when not to fight city hall."

Remarking on the sparse walls of his office, Toner wrote, "His office suggests this confidence. The walls lack the rows of diplomas, certificates, awards, proclamations and other props of official identity, hinting that if you don't know who Kenneth Thompson is, then you may be in the wrong office."

Discussing his fiscal conservativeness Thompson was quoted as saying, "Never in the time that I have been here has the city had to issue tax anticipation notes or borrow against anticipated revenues for operating purposes...If that is municipal parsimony, I'm inclined to plead guilty."

At the time of the article, Thompson was twenty-three years into his tenure, which Toner likened to playing right tackle for the Green Bay Packers for forty-three years.

Former commissioner Gil Waters was quoted as saying that he liked Thompson, just not as a city manager. Waters felt that "Thompson's goal has been simply to maintain 'the status quo.'"

Former mayor William Overton, president of Sarasota Federal Savings & Loan Association, praised Thompson for keeping the city "fiscally healthy." According to Overton, Thompson's tight-fistedness did not cause a deprivation of services for city residents.

Regrouping

Coincidentally, while Toner was gathering information for his article, newly elected mayor Tony Saprito faced his first official crisis—a May Day walkout of city bus drivers.

Ted Watts, representing the drivers at the commission chambers, confronted the mayor and commissioners with their demands. Thompson, who sat on Saprito's left, conferred back and forth, Thompson practicing his trademark "mumblese." After a half hour, Watts left satisfied, and the drivers returned to work, the success of the meeting attributed to Thompson, "who was a soothing influence."

Elmer Berkel remembers Thompson fondly, recalling, "He was one of the most brilliant men I have ever met." A two-term mayor, and twice elected to the commission, Berkel served Sarasota from 1974 through 1979. He was from the public service sector, paid by the school board as a psychologist and an administrator, not a downtown businessman like most of the commissioners who preceded him.

He recalled that in those days the commissioners all had full-time jobs working forty or fifty hours or more a week, plus their family responsibilities. Because of time constraints, they all relied heavily on Thompson, and they valued his advice.

At city hall, there was a business-oriented philosophy of how the city should grow and be governed, and the commission and Thompson shared the same philosophy, making their work together all the easier.

Berkel said that Thompson did not rule with an iron fist. It was just that commissioners had "such busy lives that they deferred to his judgment. And he delivered. He got things done."

What Berkel regretted most about his time on the commission was the amount of time his mayor/commission responsibilities took away from his family.

In those days, commissioners still were not paid. The mayor received $50 per month for out-of-pocket costs such as travel to ribbon-cutting ceremonies or to give speeches. Soon, the stipend was upped to $100, with the vice-mayor getting $75.

Nor, said Berkel, did the commissioners have a private office; the mayor and all the commissioners shared one office and tried to make appointments when no one else was using it.

One of Berkel's proudest accomplishments was his push for a form of affirmative action in city government. He spoke to Thompson about it, and Thompson agreed with him. He put the matter on the commission agenda, and it was passed.

Hand-in-hand with affirmative action was Thompson's desire to work with Berkel on getting in-service training for the department heads to increase their people skills.

Berkel thought that the Ed James story of how the library became integrated underscored the quiet and efficient manner in which Thompson operated. A simple phone call had prevented what could have been a major problem.

Berkel felt that the outward migration of businesses from downtown affected Sarasota no differently than any other 1970s southern communities, adding that Thompson would grant no special deals to anyone on rezoning.

According to Berkel, in the early '70s, Thompson and his planning board pushed for and got the downtown area of Sarasota totally rezoned.

Berkel said the density in the area from Fruitville Road to Tenth Street was increased to allow for more development, while density in the downtown core was decreased, thereby increasing property values.

He indicated that Thompson and his planning board did 75 to 85 percent of the work themselves and, in his view, their plan accounts for the look of today's Sarasota.

Berkel used the term "soft Sunshine Law" to describe how business was conducted during his first stint as commissioner. The more stringent version of the Government in the Sunshine Law, now one of the strongest in the nation, would come later.

"It was easier to conduct business in those days. Everyone would pile into the Thompson Pontiac, drive out to the Bobby Jones Club House and sit around a table and discuss the forthcoming commission meeting. There was no audience to play up to, so passions were not as strong; and Thompson was a calming influence."

One of Thompson's biggest supporters—both then and, to his memory, now—was commissioner and three-time mayor Fred Soto.

Soto, whom the *Herald* called the most verbal and active mayor Sarasota had ever had, spent half of his working day at city hall and knew Thompson

Regrouping

Looking east at Main Street and Orange Avenue, 1968. The Sarasota Bank & Trust Company, with Emmet Addy as its president, replaced a bus depot here in 1956. To the rear, construction is underway for the Ellis Building. *Sarasota County History Center, Pete Esthus Collection.*

well. "The greatest," he said of him. "No one will ever touch him. He was a powerful man, and there will never be another one like him."

Soto, who served two years on the city planning board and then on the commission from 1969 until 1981, recalled those 1970s days when downtown had fallen on hard times. Sears and JC Penney left, creating a shopping void. "I credit Thompson for saving downtown," Soto said. "He made it what it is today."

The downtown bay front and the keys were enjoying a resurgence in building activity, most visibly the twenty-five-story Plymouth Harbor on Coon Key, an award-winning design by Frank Folsom Smith and Louis F. Schneider. It was the tallest residential structure in Florida at the time, requiring 2 million pounds of concrete for its slab. But the city's central core east of Gulfstream continued its slide and was showing its age.

Not only did Sears, Roebuck and Co. and JC Penney leave Main Street, but also during the 1960s and into the 1970s a succession of changes had taken place downtown: the old Colonial Hotel at Main Street and Palm Avenue was closed in 1962; most of the south side of lower Main Street, including Badgers Drugstore, was razed in 1964 in favor of a parking lot; the Orange Blossom Hotel closed in 1965 to be reopened in 1968 as less glamorous retirement apartments; the Ritz Theatre closed in 1965 and the Florida Theatre closed in 1971; the Hotel Sarasota, the city's first skyscraper, was cited as a fire hazard and closed in 1971, to be remodeled as an office building; the DeSoto Hotel on upper Main Street near the train station was razed; and on First Street, across from city hall, the perennially popular Plaza Restaurant, watering hole and gathering place for two generations of diners, drinkers and deal-makers served its last meal in 1974.

Soto recalled, "Thompson had given the problems of a deteriorating downtown a lot of thought. And he felt the best way to rejuvenate the area was to rezone downtown for condominiums, and that started the downtown resurgence. Condos are still selling," he added.

In 1972, the center of downtown at Five Points was boosted with the addition of the headquarters of United First Federal, a twelve-story behemoth built on the parking lot where Badgers Drugs, the "Store of the Town," had been.

Across the street, the Palmer Bank was remodeled and updated with a modern façade over its blond bricks, as were many of the small retail outlets that remained along Main Street.

Former mayor and commissioner Rita Roehr, who served Sarasota for ten years between 1981 and 1989, said, "The plan to attract condominium development that Thompson formulated with his staff turned out great; it accounts for the Sarasota we have today."

Thompson saw the economic vitality of downtown tied to upscale condominiums, but not at any cost. A project slated for Gulfstream Avenue that was not deemed suitable was a super-size building called Marina Towers. The building permit for it, issued in 1973 under the old zoning code, was revoked by the city in favor of the new code. The Chicago-based developer took the case to court and, after a four-year battle, finally won.

In 1977, a new development group took over, calling its proposed project Admirals Walk, which never panned out.

Finally, in 1980, Bay Plaza, a mixed-use condominium, was begun on the site. This is what Thompson and the city commission were striving for.

Regrouping

Looking over Sarasota Bay and Gulfstream Avenue, 1974. Note that Bird Key, upper right, is fully developed, and condominiums have started filling in along Gulfstream Avenue, starting to be known as "condo row." *C. Kennedy Photo, Sarasota County History Center.*

Another of Tim Seibert's designs, it was situated directly across the street from Marina Jack. The $20 million building was to include a grocery store, a drugstore and other retail establishments to service the area's new condo and apartment dwellers.

Constructed by the Skandia Group of New York, which had done the Heron Bay Club, the fourteen-story condominium with one hundred units was the pinnacle of downtown luxury, with a doorman, special security services, housekeeping staff and even a concierge.

A city resolution was passed that slightly backed down the requirement that 20 percent of the building be devoted to commercial space and allowed Thompson to handle whatever issues might arise without the need of the developers to come before the city commission.

By the time the project was opened in 1983, it joined numerous other condominium and apartment buildings, with Gulfstream Avenue becoming known as "condo row."

When Thompson retired in 1988, Gulfstream Avenue would have the following condominiums lining the way: One Watergate, Bay Plaza,

THE RISE OF SARASOTA

Thompson on his last day as city manager, atop the Bay Plaza Condominium overlooking the town that he helped to create. *Courtesy Barbara Thompson.*

Gulf Stream Towers, Dolphin Tower, Saint Regis Condominiums, Regency House Apartments, Royal Saint Andrew Apartments, Versailles Apartments and the Essex House, all a boon to what had been a struggling downtown economy.

While not everyone agreed with Thompson's fiscal conservatism, Roehr said she didn't know of anyone who did not respect him.

She recalled that he always tried to back up the commissioners, helping them solve their problems: "If a commissioner started to stumble over something at a meeting, Thompson would interject a relevant fact to keep the conversation going."

"There was talk that if they got Ken Thompson out, Sarasota would take off. Well he's out, where did we take off to?" she asked.

In 1972, part of the revitalization process called for the purchase and razing of the old Seaboard Coast Line Railway Station at Main Street and Lemon Avenue, transforming it into a pedestrian mall.

Called the Lemon Avenue Beautification Project, the mall was dedicated on July 4, 1976. Designed by West and Conyers Architects, the landscape

Regrouping

work was done by Lane L. Marshall and won the municipal landscape award from the Manasota Nurserymen and Growers Association.

The year 1972 also saw the adoption of a tree protection ordinance—too late for the memorial oak trees—and the requirement that construction along beachfront property at Lido Beach had to be 150 feet back from the high-water line.

Soto recalled that most of Thompson's employees seemed to love him, and he them: "Everyone at city hall got along fine; it just worked so well."

Billy Robinson, who started in the city auditor's office in 1979 and retired as the city auditor and clerk in 2010, said the staff at city hall worked closely together in Thompson's day. "The city was very much like a family," he said. He was like the father image, and everyone respected him.

That would seem to be borne out by the long tenures of his subordinates. According to the *Times*, who listed city officials and their years of service, all totaled, by 1986 eleven department heads were eligible to retire. Mrs. Elizabeth Jackson faithfully served for nearly twenty-five years as Thompson's administrative assistant before retiring.

For some, this job longevity made for a cohesive, well-run operation; for others, it was tired blood.

Soto recalled that one of the signal events of the 1970s was the purchase of the Arvida property on North Lido Beach, for which Thompson pushed hard.

In the late 1960s, Ted Sperling headed up the effort to keep the beautiful piece of property in its pristine condition, to be enjoyed by the beach-going public.

Arvida had wanted to develop the sixty-five-acre parcel of land with homes and high-rise condominiums much like the south end of Longboat Key. But after a battle with Save Our Bays and other interested groups to prevent it, it decided to sell.

As the matter came to a head, Thompson had a proposed purchase contract drawn up to present to the Arvida Corp.

On March 15, 1977, the citizens voted by a four-to-one margin to issue a $1.35 million general obligation bond to enable the purchase. After the bond passed, Commissioner Sperling called it the "end of an eight-year odyssey."

The Rise of Sarasota

Looking up lower Main Street toward Five Points and the remodeled Palmer Bank, circa 1972. Note that one-way traffic was tried for a while but discontinued. *Sarasota County History Center, Bill Blackstone Collection.*

There were at least half a dozen other parcels of property on North Lido that needed to be purchased from private individuals, and acquiring them was a slow process.

Another piece of waterfront property that Commissioner Sperling pushed for the city to buy was the old Florida Power and Light (FPL) site on Sarasota Bay at Tenth Street. In April 1977, he called for the city to formally inform FPL of the city's intent to purchase the land.

The post–World War II power plant there had been closed since 1965. Thompson, agreeing with Sperling, wanted the site to be used as a public park, a place where boats could be launched.

Ultimately, the property was acquired, with Mayor Soto presenting a check to FPL representative R.W. Kerlikoske on August 2, 1979.

The site was formally dedicated on April 27, 1986, as Centennial Park to mark the 100th anniversary of the failed Scot colony.

The dedication featured a fireworks display, a team of skydivers and the presentation of a centennial flag to John Browning, a descendant of one of the original Scot families.

Regrouping

According to Paul Thorpe, former president of the Downtown Association of Sarasota, it was Thompson who first gave the green light for the Downtown Farmers' Market on Lemon Avenue, popular with tourists and residents alike to this day and a major draw on Saturday mornings.

Thorpe recalled that in 1979 he approached Thompson with the idea, and after a discussion, and with only a handshake to seal the deal, Thompson brought the matter before the city commission and had it approved. Thorpe said no paperwork was involved.

Thorpe, who is often called "Mr. Downtown" for all he has done to rejuvenate the area, had been the assistant vice-president in charge of marketing for the Palmer Bank at Five Points, and he knew that Thompson was the go-to guy to get a project off the ground.

"Thompson always encouraged the merchants to become involved in projects that would draw people downtown," Thorpe said.

He also credited Thompson for his role in facilitating the Suncoast Offshore Grand Prix. Noting Thompson was a boatman, Thorpe recalled that the original route called for the racers to go under the Ringling Bridge and through Big Pass. That popular, high-visibility route was halted because of noise complaints.

Two accolades were accorded to Thompson in 1979. The Sarasota-Manatee Engineering Society and the Myakka Chapter of the Florida Engineering Society named him Engineer of the Year.

That honor was followed in May with an award from the Veterans of Foreign Wars as its Man of the Year.

Both achievements were recognized by United States congressman Andy Ireland, who wrote to him, "The honor is a tribute to your leadership, dedication and hard work."

Ending the decade of the 1970s, on December 15, 1979, the Tony Saprito Fishing Pier was dedicated to honor the long-serving mayor/commissioner. Saprito, who had served the city for twenty years, lobbied hard for the pier for several years, spurred on when an angler was killed fishing off of the Ringling Bridge. It was expected that fishing on the bridge would be banned, and the reported $250,000 pier would offer a safe alternative.

The Department of Transportation posted "No Fishing" signs on the bridge, but the city often turned a blind eye to the fishermen who still preferred it to the pier.

The ever-popular Farmers' Market on Lemon Avenue and State Street was founded with a handshake between Paul Thorpe and Ken Thompson. It has been a popular Saturday morning downtown event for over thirty years. *Photo by Jeff LaHurd.*

As Thompson put it, "We take our problems on a priority basis. The police have higher-priority items than to give special enforcement to fishing."

6
"I DO"

Thompson's marriage to Virginia ended in divorce in 1965. His workaholic habits played a role, and their son, Charles, indicated that they probably married too young and had dissimilar personalities. He said of his mother, "She loved people, parties, gaiety; but she was neither stupid nor silly."

Thompson was more reticent. Charles continued, "While they shared a common interest in art and clever people, I think the temperamental difference which was exacerbated as Ken's public role increased, wore her down."

She remarried to Dexter French, a Miami attorney who was an old friend of the Thompsons, and in 1973 they moved to England.

Thompson met a new love, Barbara Davies Johnson, in 1967.

Barbara mentioned to a friend that she was having trouble with the wiring of a light fixture, and later the friend sent an electrical engineer she knew named Ken Thompson to fix it.

Johnson was then a single mother, raising her young daughter, Laura.

After two years of dating, they were wed on May 27, 1969.

The wedding day photo in the paper over the cut line "Marital Bliss for City Manager" showed the handsome couple holding hands, Barbara in a lovely white dress wearing white gloves and a pill box hat and Thompson outfitted in a black tuxedo, white shirt, bow tie and boutonniere. Standing with them was Laura, holding a bouquet of flowers, and her young cousin, Fraser Davies.

The Thompson family—Barbara, Laura and Kenneth—take a look at one of Thompson's drawings. Not pictured is son Charles, who was teaching at Oxford College when this picture was taken. *Courtesy Barbara Thompson.*

Thompson bonded with Laura immediately and adopted her shortly after the marriage. The three formed a loving, close-knit trio.

The honeymoon was a brief flying trip to Abaco in the Bahamas, leaving directly after the Thursday morning ceremony and back on Saturday.

They lived at Thompson's Harbor Acres home on Hillview Drive. As Thompson recalled, he bought the property for $4,000 and commissioned plans for the new home from Sarasota School of Architecture architect William Zimmerman.

He loved the bay-front property, which he called the most convenient place in Sarasota. He told Anne Proffitt that he was attracted to the area by the bay. "I had my first sailboat in 1924, sixteen-footer. Since then, I have had nine sailboats. The one I sold last year [1991] was a thirty-eight-foot center cockpit sloop. However, I still have my Sunfish."

He was able to sail the large sloop singlehandedly, saying it was the best exercise he ever got.

"I Do"

His son, Ken, remembered that his father was at his happiest behind the wheel of one of his sailboats out on the bay: "He sailed right up until the end, even when it wasn't safe for him to take the small Sunfish sailboat out anymore by himself; it just was not in his nature to give it up."

Much of the job stress was relieved through his hobbies, exercise and artwork. He started drawing in high school and was an inveterate doodler at commission meetings. Mrs. Thompson could tell how a particular evening went by the amount and type of doodles that came home with him. She indicated that he did not discuss city hall business, sparing her and the family from the high anxiety the job could generate, especially at the end of his time in office when he was under pressure to step down. During those commission meetings, she attended to offer moral support to her beleaguered husband.

Ken said his father never complained at home about work or what happened with the city commission. Even when beset by ouster attempts, he kept his calm at home—his island of tranquility in a sometimes rough sea of commission bickering.

Thompson was sixty-one years old when Ken was born, older than most fathers. But it did not prevent him from being a fully involved father in Ken's and Laura's lives. "He spent a lot of time with me when I was growing up. He was right out there showing me how to play baseball, basketball, sail, et cetera," said Ken.

Laura remembers her father pulling into the driveway, still in his suit and tie, and running outside to have him play baseball with her in the front yard.

On the occasions when he had a particularly full Monday night commission meeting to prepare for, Barbara would bring the children down to city hall in the evening, and Laura would sit on his desk and "watch him work his magic with city business."

Former mayor Cohen, who worked with Thompson for ten years, commented once that Thompson was a man with "a brain and a heart."

That was especially true at home. Laura called him a born teacher, a patient, gentle man who was her guiding force; the reason, she said, that she became a teacher herself—"to be able to pass on to other generations the gift of learning," as he had done for her.

Ken recalled that his father particularly enjoyed building things with him and his friends. Thompson's workshop was well outfitted with all sorts of equipment, and he would spend hours with the neighborhood children building small items, especially little wooden sailboats that they would take to the backyard dock and race in the bay.

Thompson and his second son, Kenneth, enjoying a meal and a glass of iced tea together. Kenneth recalled that his father was a loving and kind man who instilled in him the value of education. *Courtesy Barbara Thompson.*

Ken thought it gave an insight into his father's humanity that he told him to always see the good in people and draw that out. "He always had a kind word to say."

Todd Thomas, one of Ken's best friends, was taken under the Thompson household wing. Thompson always welcomed Todd in the home with the greeting, "Hullo Toddious!"

Thompson became a father figure to him. In a school paper, he wrote about his relationship with the Thompsons in general and Mr. Thompson in particular: "He will always listen to everything you have to say while waiting until your last words are spoken before he speaks. His words are well chosen, simple and full of knowledge."

When Ken was hosted as a Brazilian exchange student during his junior year, the Thompsons paid for Todd's trip there for a visit. Mr. Thompson told him not to worry about paying him back monetarily—that by becoming

"I Do"

a success in life and learning something from everything he did would be payment enough.

One of the stories Thompson told Ken to underscore public service was that back in his baseball-playing days, he and his teammates would pick up trash on the field and stuff it into their pockets: "Just because something wasn't your job didn't mean it shouldn't get done."

As for baseball, Thompson never regretted not pursuing it as a profession, figuring that if he had, he might have spent his whole career in the minor leagues.

Thompson began drawing when he was in high school and continued throughout his life. His wife, Barbara, could tell how successful or how stressful a commission meeting was for him by the amount and type of doodles he brought home. *Courtesy Barbara Thompson.*

A Christmas card drawn by Thompson. *Courtesy Barbara Thompson.*

His artistic passion found expression in his wire art. As a trained electrical engineer, he was adept at bending wire and designed some fascinating pieces, usually with a nautical theme, which he gave away to friends or displayed at local art galleries. He fashioned a giant heart in colored lights and wires to put out during the Christmas season.

The Thompsons led a quiet life together, socializing with close friends, going out on the bay in his sailboat, occasionally taking weekend mini-vacations in his leased Cessna plane and involving themselves in their children's school and social lives.

The office was close enough that he could drive home for lunch, which he did whenever possible.

There was no television in the living room, and after supper together, evenings were spent reading, reciting poetry and listening to music.

Friday night was playtime in the household for the neighborhood children, who would come over for recreation with the Thompson children, playing games and dancing on the table in the center of the room.

"I Do"

Ken said his father instilled in all his children the value of education—that it was the expectation in the household that a college education was paramount and that a full life was not about making money. Achievement in the arts or sciences was much more important than being merely wealthy. His father would have loved him to get a PhD in philosophy.

Ken opted for a degree in business administration from the University of Texas–Austin and received a master of business administration from Northwestern University.

Laura, now Laura Thompson DeUnger, a teacher at Southside Elementary School for over twenty-four years, is also an artist.

On at least one occasion, she and Thompson put on a father/daughter art show and reception at the Strawberry Hill Gallery in the United States Garage, he showing his wire sculptures and she her pastel and watercolor paintings. She received a bachelor's degree from the Ringling School of Art and Design and a master's degree in education from the University of South Florida.

Charles, who moved to England in 1968, was a fellow of the Oxford Centre for Management Studies, an institute of Oxford University.

In correspondence to me, he recalled his father's great natural curiosity about the environment: "I knew about beach berms, juvenile lime stones, iron pans, sink holes, recharge areas/the 'green swamp,' phosphate deposits...long before high school thanks to Ken."

He said his father was a natural scientist who gave him a full ration of kindness and more. And as with his later children, Thompson took time each afternoon when he came home from the office for fielding and batting practice with Charles.

Charles's memories of his parents' time together in Sarasota before the divorce were long drives to the interior to look at the county.

He recalled that his father's middle-aged dream was to "ultimately retire to a shack in the islands south of Sanibel with a traditional sailing boat and become a beach comber."

Charles ended by saying, "I remember him as intensely intelligent, intellectually disciplined and widely curious. I owe him."

By the time Laura was old enough to date in high school, her father advised that her boyfriend (and future husband) had better learn to sail. He took him out on the bay in his sailboat and taught him how.

Granddaughters Alexandra DeUnger and Amanda DeUnger Lewis spent a significant amount of time with their grandparents. On the days

THE RISE OF SARASOTA

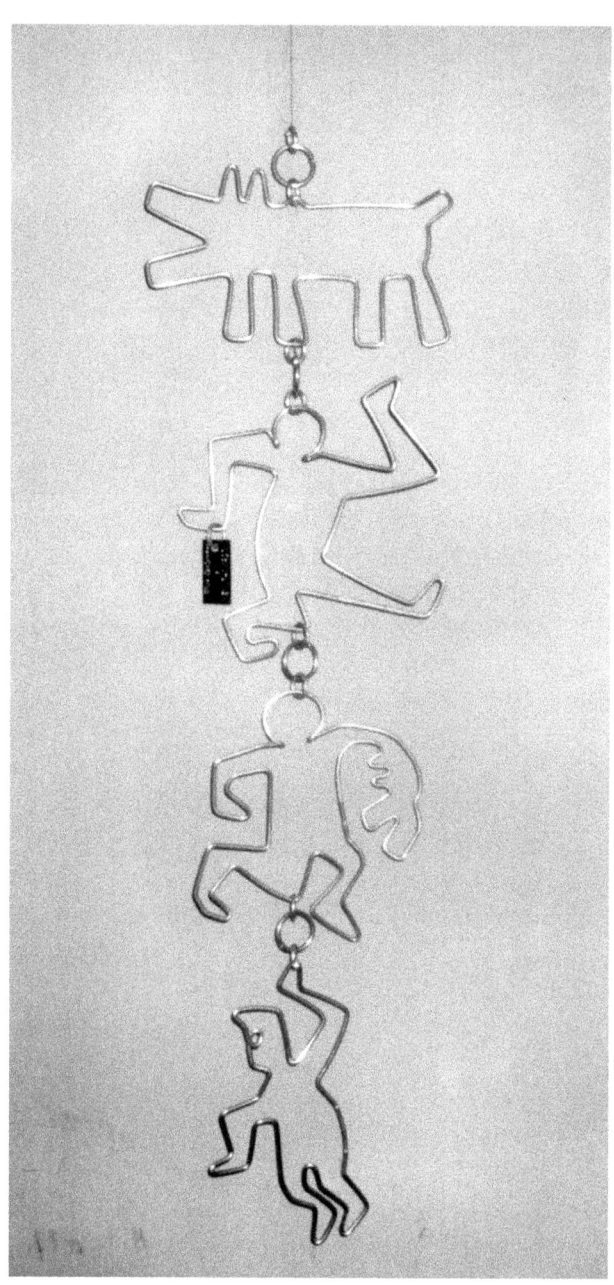

As an electrical engineer, bending wire came naturally to Thompson. He never sold his works of wire art but gave them to friends or displayed them in galleries. One of his nautical-themed creations is on permanent display at Mote Marine Laboratory on City Island. *Courtesy Barbara Thompson.*

"I Do"

their mother taught at Southside School, they were dropped off at the Thompsons', who looked after them.

Both have fond memories. Alexandra said that because of her grandfather's love of art, she recalled that her childhood "revolved around colored pencils, paint and clay."

It seemed an idyllic home for a child to go to—a combination learning center and playhouse. As early as seven years old, Thompson took Amanda on the Sunfish to teach her how to sail, how to make a tepee out of bamboo in the backyard, how to make perfume out of flowers and plants around the yard and even how to pick oysters. He also taught her some rudimentary Spanish and Cuban card games he remembered from his Pine Island days.

Every day that they were with their grandfather, he gave them encouragement to pursue their goals and instilled in them a thirst for knowledge that evidently took hold. Amanda graduated from Florida State University in the honors program with a degree in psychology and is currently studying at Johns Hopkins University to be a pediatric nurse practitioner.

Alexandra is a senior at Pine View School.

The girls called him "Papa," and Amanda remembered that each and every day he would put her on his lap and tell her, "No matter what anyone in this world tells you, never forget how beautiful you are inside and out."

She wrote of him, "I will continuously thank my grandfather for the joyous memories and life lessons that will carry on to my children. I will continue to look up to him for his passion and love that he had for the city of Sarasota, his family and his friends."

7

TRYING TO HOLD ON

The 1980s

To me the quality of living here in Sarasota has been something worthy of being preserved.
—*Ken Thompson*

In 1984, his thirty-fourth year in office, the newspaper articles about Thompson and his view of the city—what it had been and, importantly, what it would become—were akin to State of the City messages.

With each year, the gorilla in the room, his retirement date, became larger, fueled by speculation that he was slowing down.

He was now seventy-four years old, and to counter the notion that he was not up to the task, newspaper stories and magazine articles showed him busy at work at his office, working out on his front-yard trampoline or sailing one of his boats. A front-page photo in the *Herald* showed him aloft, bouncing on the trampoline, with the cut line: "The Boss Still Has the Jump on His Foes."

An article by Jud Magrin in the *Herald* said that while some unnamed staffers thought too much city business had gone unattended to, others sought his approval on all but the mundane tasks.

City purchasing director Robert Gerkin spoke for the Thompson supporters at city hall when he said, "My loyalties lie with him—period."

Thompson's view of what Sarasota needed to keep pace with growth was tied to improving the infrastructure: "Our biggest problem is to whip our wastewater system into line; especially the sewer pipes so they don't overflow when we have heavy rains."

He saw the Planning Board, which he started two years after taking office, as one of the more important city boards. He was not anti-growth, but it was paramount to him that it be properly controlled and channeled.

In 1952, he had written about the community's unique art and culture venues that could not be bought with dollars: "We may be a little jealous of them, and fear that too great an influx of new people might threaten this little cornered market."

He did not want to sacrifice the unique ambiance to unfettered development. It was the "fear of losing ground to those who may not care for the charm of Sarasota and who may wish it to become something else."

He said newcomers should be "sited in such a way that they don't affect or utilize the scarce assets." His answer was "to increase density of the existing urbanized area, unless we're going to carve up more farmlands."

Thompson favored the more complex zoning structure of Sarasota suggested by Regional Urban Design Assistance Team (R/UDAT); he called them good professionals who knew what they were doing.

In an interview with David Steiling of Sarasota's *Times*, he said, "Part of the argument used against me is that I'm 'Old Florida' to which I agree…I'm out of tune with the present wave of creating the 'festive marketplace,' the new buzz-word for this city."

As to his retirement, the *Herald* reported that the Sarasota County Civic League had initiated a charter review process to mandate a retirement age of seventy-five for charter officials like Thompson.

City commissioner Dean Mason said it should be up to the commission, not the person, when someone should retire. Mason said Thompson should be put on a retirement schedule.

Three years and out was offered by Thompson, which some thought was too long.

Not everyone. Former mayor Fred Soto was against the seventy-five-year age limit, saying, "If a person is doing a good job and still has a lot to offer, why force retirement?"

Soto added, "There is no question in my mind he is one of the great city managers of all time. He has a level of honesty you don't find in a person at his level."

Soto wanted the commission to offer Thompson a three-year contract. Many businessmen were also pro-Thompson, causing some in the commission to resent the influence of local businessmen on commission decisions.

While the negotiations were going on, Waldo Proffitt wrote that with only a fifteen-month time gap separating Thompson from the commission, and with Thompson giving the city thirty-six years of valuable service, "what's the rush?"

He likened Thompson to "a running back who may have lost a half step of speed but more than makes up for that in his unique knowledge of what has happened to this city and its government in the past third of a century."

For all practical purposes, Thompson wrote the play book.

Magrin noted, "While all the talk and printed words flow, Thompson...smiles and says, 'I've been to my doctor. Everything is great.'"

In June 1985, the *Herald* reported that one of Thompson's top men, Al Eddy, city engineer since 1966, was leaving city government. Thompson called him one of the best, most competent engineers he'd ever known.

Eddy joined in recent retirement police chief Francis Scott, who served from 1959 to 1982, and former Parks and Recreation Department head Howard O. "Red" Ermisch, on the job from 1966 to January 1985.

Thompson was not inclined to follow them into retirement. But whether he wanted it or not, retirement was close at hand.

The last city commission that Thompson worked with was composed of Rita Roehr, Bill Kline, Lou Ann Palmer, Kerry Kirschner and Fredd Atkins.

In 1984, after decades of on-again, off-again attempts to remove him from office, commissioners became upset with him because he was slow to notify them that a citation had been issued against the city by the Environmental Protection Agency and, later, because they were kept in the dark concerning cost overruns in the sewage treatment expansion program.

Thompson was also under fire by the NAACP. Its local president, John Rivers, was critical of the police department's handling of issues in the Newtown Community. Rivers reportedly criticized Thompson for not being sensitive to minority concerns.

The previous month, Thompson asked Chief Earl Parker to complete a report on how the department could mend its relations with the black community. The *Herald* reported that the department expanded the Neighborhood Watch Program, enhanced recruiting of black officers, increased human relations training and took several other steps to alleviate the problems. There was also talk of putting a precinct house in Newtown. Rivers, however, wanted Thompson fired.

Thompson indicated in an interview with Rick Barry that there were still many projects he needed to finish before he would consider retirement. He listed the controversial spray irrigation system to end the dumping of treated sewage into Sarasota Bay, a $19,000,000 bond issue and downtown redevelopment.

Thompson mused that in thirty months, between his jobs in Miami Beach and Sarasota, he would have put in fifty years of public service, which he termed a nice mark.

Commissioners Kline, Kirschner and Palmer seemed exasperated. According to a Jon Dietz article in the *Herald*, Palmer was quoted as saying, "The debate over Thompson is not working out."

City Attorney Richard Taylor told the commissioners that it would take a unanimous vote to remove Thompson or a majority vote if there was just cause. They would have to put the reasons for dismissal in writing, provide it to Thompson and hold a public hearing.

Thompson, who still enjoyed the backing of Roehr and Atkins, said both he and the commission had certain rights and that he was not submitting his resignation.

Taylor was quoted that he was not a special prosecutor. The commission would have to provide a reason to remove Thompson.

According to the transcript of the city commission meeting of September 16, 1985, a long discussion ensued among the commissioners about the transition of city government after Thompson left, whether by choice or vote by them.

Kirschner suggested a national search with the idea of the replacement for Thompson to take place in the middle of the 1986–87 budget year.

Kline thought that was too long a time: "From a management standpoint, Kerry, does it make sense to drag out that kind of a selection process too long."

Palmer indicated that the whole process should not take six months.

Thompson had lobbied the commissioners earlier that day, offering to retire in two and a half years.

City Attorney Taylor advised, "I think what I'm hearing is that effective January 1 of 1987 you want a new city manager in place...uh, that sounds like it is a mandatory retirement to me and on what grounds? I don't see the grounds for it."

Atkins, the first African American to serve on the commission, asked, "With this whole situation, I...I didn't quite understand or appreciate how we came to this predicament we're in tonight. Everybody up here, squirming [laughter]."

He went on, "I'm saying that anytime you start talking about setting a date for somebody to leave you in effect [are] firing them."

Atkins also believed that Thompson was still up to the task: "Ken has the best interest of Sarasota at heart. I think that his plan is a sound plan for getting things done that are already in process, and I think that we need to seriously consider using the time and the man and his experience."

Each of the commissioners gave Thompson high marks on his service to the city.

As Kirschner put it, "I think the purpose of this was not a condemnation of Ken. I think we, as citizens of the city of Sarasota, we should feel most fortunate that we've had a person like Ken serve us for so many years, and I think the beauty about this is Ken's desire to see a well-planned transition on behalf of the city of Sarasota."

Kline added, "I would agree with you, Kerry, and certainly I share those same feelings...everyone has a great deal of love and respect for Ken and appreciation of his many years of service to the city."

Roehr said she was willing to accept the two-and-a-half-year offer from Thompson, which Kline thought too long.

Palmer stressed that they were not talking about firing Thompson: "I honestly don't think that anybody at this commission has any stomach for firing anybody... There're obviously not five votes [required to terminate Thompson]."

At the end of the lengthy meeting, Kirschner moved "that we go through search procedures with an effective date of January 1, 1987."

The motion was seconded by Palmer.

Kline interjected, "For a new city manager, not for the search procedure. Effective date of January 1, 1987. Is for a new city manager, not for a new search procedure."

Roehr: "Is that your motion?"

Kirschner: "Yes."

The motion was approved by Kirschner, Kline and Palmer. Atkins and Roehr voted no.

Roehr said she did not want him "railroaded out," that after his many years of service she wanted him to have the respect he deserved. It was her wish to pursue a compromise.

Ultimately, it would be negotiated that Thompson would leave office on July 1, 1987, help his replacement and be kept on the payroll with his accumulated vacation time until February 1, 1988.

In a recent interview, Kirschner, now head of the Argus Foundation, said it was not so much that they were trying to get Thompson out as it was to plan a succession. If something happened, they did not want to be on a sinking ship with no one at the helm: "We were trying to get him to recognize that an orderly transition needed to be in place."

Kirschner, who is currently advocating for a strong city manager, said, "Thompson was the poster child for city managers."

"Ken's life was the city of Sarasota. He was part of the fabric of the community." Kirschner called him "very even handed and balanced."

He remembered Thompson was cautious about taking federal dollars because there was always a time limit on the money. "If the federal government said we can give you enough money to increase your police department by 10 percent, Ken would ask, 'Well, how are we going to pay for these officers in three years when the money stops coming?' He always looked into the future."

Kirschner also recalled that Thompson was not bashful about informing the commissioners about the "delineation" of responsibilities. If someone stepped over the line, Thompson would assuredly inform that commissioner, "That's not your job. That's my job."

Illustrating Thompson's ability to get things done, Kirschner related a story of cutting the red tape to acquire approval of a new Publix grocery store.

As Kirschner's story goes, the proposed store straddled both the city and the county, and George W. Jenkins, who founded Publix, was having a difficult time dealing with both the city and county governments' layers of building codes and inspections.

Jenkins put in a call to local grocer Ted Morton, whom he knew from Morton's days of being a salesman for the National Biscuit Company.

He and Morton met for lunch, and Jenkins spelled out his ongoing problems and wondered if it was always so difficult to get things done in Sarasota. Did Morton know anyone who could help?

Morton said he would see what he could do and called Thompson later, explaining the situation.

Thompson promised to look into it. A day or so later, Thompson called Morton back and said the problem had been resolved; after talking to the county administrator (probably his friend and one-time assistant Ed Hoyt), the two decided expediency should prevail over bureaucracy, and he ordered his public works department to move the city limit sign a few yards so that all of the Publix store was within the city limits.

Kirschner ended by saying, "Ken Thompson was Mr. Sarasota."

Trying to Hold On

Thompson's replacement was David Sollenberger, a genial, soft-spoken gentleman; a former teacher who had led the cities of Watsonville, California; Vallejo, California; and Winona, Minnesota, before coming to Sarasota.

Palmer, who was first elected in 1982 and served until 1991 and again from 2001 to 2009, and served five terms as mayor, called Thompson the "sixth city commissioner."

She agreed with Berkel that he was "an extraordinarily brilliant man."

Palmer recalled, "The man was powerful and influential." She cited his "incredible background and professional expertise in so many different areas: water treatment, zoning, planning. He seemed to understand all the details."

"When Ken made a decision, it was usually carried out by the commission," she added.

He had a thorough knowledge of the Advance Wastewater Treatment program, and although it happened on his replacement's watch, Thompson, she said, had been the one pushing for it.

She indicated that he was solidly behind bringing the city's zoning code up to date and worked hard with his staff to that end.

Of Thompson's departure, she said, "Basically, I said to Ken, it was his time."

Thompson was quoted in the *Herald* as saying, "They apparently believe that the city needs to change its direction, from being just a nice place to live to one of dynamic economic progress with…the redevelopment of downtown and the opening up of other arteries."

Both Mrs. Thompson and her son, Ken, said that he was not bitter about being forced out as city manager. It was not in his nature.

When Sollenberger arrived, Thompson penned a letter of welcome to his successor. Noting that Sollenberger had the fine qualities of a model city manager, he went on, "Yours is a call to apply your skills to the management needs of a very special city, one that I have nurtured for thirty-seven years."

He gave the new city manager an overview of Sarasota's attributes and described the city's special needs: the environment, sandy beaches, bays, wetlands and water resources that needed protection or the city would lose its special character. He ended, "Treat this little city gently and she will respond properly."

Thompson, who had always pushed the cultural amenities of Sarasota as a way to improve the city's economy, hoped that Sollenberger would do the same. As Thompson once put it, "It's correct to say that I'm manipulating artistic elements for the purpose of enhancing the economic base of this city."

And he would. According to the *Herald*, "Sollenberger has said he will continue efforts to enhance the cultural and artistic characteristics of the city."

Palmer said that for the year or so between Sollenberger's arrival from Minnesota and Thompson's departure, Thompson was useful to Sollenberger, who knew nothing of Sarasota, helping to bring his successor up to speed.

Thompson's secretary, Carolyn Hereford, who started working for him in 1979, helped with the transition, working for both men. She had gained a vast amount of city knowledge by going through the old files to acclimate herself to the job when she first started with Thompson.

When Thompson left, Hereford became Sollenberger's administrative assistant.

Local planner and planning consultant Bruce Franklin, who has worked in Sarasota for over thirty years and often dealt with city hall as four city managers have come and gone, indicated, "Sollenberger slowly matriculated out many of the Thompson regime."

According to Franklin, "Thompson was a 'Let's get it done kind of guy.' I always felt that if I got into a bind with a project, I could go to Ken and he would listen to the problem and call in the appropriate director and try to smooth things out."

Franklin offered, "Nothing ever took ten years to get done during Thompson's tenure." Offering as examples of recent drawn-out projects: the Selby Library, the third Ringling Bridge, the downtown bus transfer station and the Palm Avenue Garage Redevelopment project.

"But things were different," he added. "Commissioners served out of their civic duty and were not into micro managing as they are today."

Sollenberger went on to serve Sarasota for fourteen years, brought down, interestingly, by problems associated with the renovation of Ken Thompson's cultural icon, the Van Wezel Performing Arts Hall, which Sollenberger called his *Titanic*.

He went on to manage Plant City and was roundly applauded there for a job well done when he retired.

Trying to Hold On

On the evening of January 31, 1987, the day before his thirty-eighth anniversary as city manager, Marge Baldwin, the irrepressible president of the Tiger Bay Club and friend of Thompson, spearheaded a heartfelt goodbye tribute to Thompson at the Sahib Temple.

At the cocktail party and dinner, over two hundred well-wishers were on hand to give the long-serving and much-loved and respected city manager a proper send-off.

The Thompson family attended, swelled with pride at this outpouring of community affirmation.

Tears flowed as freely as plaudits from the city's movers and shakers: bankers, lawyers, some twenty past and present commissioners and mayors, legislators and local civic leaders.

An oversized picture of Thompson high in the air, bouncing on his trampoline, was hung for all to see.

Waldo Proffitt, the emcee for the evening, told the audience, "If you want to know what Ken Thompson has been doing for the last thirty-seven years, look around. Ken had both the vision to see what he wanted Sarasota to be and the patience to wait for the right combination of time and circumstance to move closer to the vision, one step at a time."

Gil Waters, one of the committee members who worked on the dinner plans and was a reporter with the *Sarasota Herald* when Thompson arrived in Sarasota in 1950, read from the original article he wrote quoting Thompson's promise, "When I come over, I'm coming to stay...we'll be citizens of Sarasota with all that it means."

Also on hand to speak were David Cohen, who worked so hard with Thompson to realize the Van Wezel Performing Arts Hall; George Higgins, who had first brought him to the attention of the city commission; and several others.

Judge Scheb gave a heart-felt speech, which ended, "But most of all I remember him as a compassionate, understanding, and fair-minded man with gracious simplicity—a man who was firm but fair; decisive, but not dictatorial; authoritative but never arrogant."

Let's Talk columnist Marjorie North quoted Baldwin, "We're not so tough, after all," referring to tears streaming down Thompson's cheeks.

An obviously moved Ken Thompson told the audience, "This is a wonderful city and I have a lot of wonderful friends."

The Rise of Sarasota

The Thompsons were gifted a trip to Europe valued at $9,000, but typical of Ken, he would not accept. He turned it down because, in his view, a public official could not accept such a significant gift.

On Saturday morning, June 27, 1987, Ken Thompson and Barbara went to his office for the last time. They were there to pick up his personal possessions to make way for David Sollenberger, who was going to move in on Sunday.

After thirty-seven years (accumulated leave time took him to thirty-eight years), there was not as much to remove as might have been the case. Long ago, he had eschewed the idea of hanging plaques, awards and photos of important personages.

Everything he removed fit into the small cardboard box they brought along. That and two paintings given to him by friends were taken to his car.

Barbara Thompson was sad and dreaded the trip; the finalization of it all weighed heavily on her. He was his usual stoic self and very quiet.

She had hoped that no reporters would be there, but one was, Gregory Enns, a staff writer for the *Herald*, and the Thompsons chatted briefly with him, answered his questions and were off for the short trip back to Harbor Acres, to his bay-front home, his sailboat, his trampoline and his loving family.

It was a simple ending to a complicated lifetime of achievement and service to a community he had come to love and lead more than a generation earlier.

8
NOT QUITE TIME TO SAY GOODBYE

We've always said, don't send us your industry, send us your industrialists.
—*Ken Thompson*

Ken Thompson and Sarasota were joined at the hip. He was involved in some way or another in the recommendations and decisions that had transformed a sleepy paradise into a dramatically vibrant, modern and culturally inviting city. He could not let go.

Billy Robinson said, "I think he just loved Sarasota and his job so much that he could not bear to leave."

He was a self-confessed workaholic who seldom took vacations. During his first fourteen years, he reportedly took one day off. Five more years went by before he took three more.

His away times were mostly of the extended weekend variety, flying with Barbara; the Bahamas was a favorite place, and he also managed to take time to go to California and on a short trip to England to visit his son, Charles.

At thirty-two years' service, it was estimated that he had taken just seventeen vacation days.

He told *Herald* reporter Robin Simmons, "I don't want to say the place goes to hell when I go away, which it probably doesn't...but I think it does. When I take off, the work just piles up and I know I'll have to do it anyway."

As for his staff, he encouraged vacation time. He once joked, "Instead of giving them stress pills, we give them vacations."

The Rise of Sarasota

For most seventy-eight-year-olds, after a challenging thirty-eight-year career as the head of a major organization, retiring would have come easily—a welcome respite from the stress of the daily grind.

For years, he had received the plaudits of an appreciative community, gained the respect of the many commissioners he had served and the admiration of subordinates and had a loving and devoted wife and family with whom to spend the last days of his life.

But long ago, the city of Sarasota became for Thompson the artist a canvas, and Thompson was not finished with his masterpiece. He was unwilling to put his brush and easel down.

On January 7, 1989, less than a year into his official retirement, Thompson announced his decision to seek a commission seat, saying that he wanted to make policy, not just carry it out.

Campaigning did not come easy to him. He was not a politician, not a backslapping, glad-hander at ease on the campaign trail. He was reticent, perhaps too cerebral to get his message across. He was not by nature a dynamic public speaker.

A retired city manager shaking hands with Governor "Walkin" Lawton Chiles at a reception, with Barbara looking on. *Courtesy Barbara Thompson.*

Not Quite Time to Say Goodbye

Campaign flyer for Thompson's 1989 run for the city commission in a field made up of eleven hopefuls. Former mayor Jack Gurney, who campaigned against Thompson and won, said Thompson probably would have been elected if he were ten years younger. *Courtesy Barbara Thompson.*

But like everything else he became involved in, he worked hard at it and stuck with it to the end.

Community speculation was rife that Thompson was running against Bill Kline in revenge for Kline's orchestrating Thompson's ouster. Thompson denied it.

He countered that he was not running against Kline but, rather, competing for the seat vacated by the retirement of Mayor Rita Roehr, the first woman elected to the commission and a longtime Thompson supporter. She had served three terms and voted not to replace Thompson.

Of course, he ran on his many years of experience, advocated quality growth that did not tax existing taxpayers for infrastructure and that was environmentally acceptable. He supported long-range planning and was against local government entering into leases with private enterprise unless it was essential for public service.

His campaign slogan was: "Good Government Is No Accident, It Requires the Finest People."

A political advertisement pictured him with his family sitting together on their lawn: VOTE FOR HONESTY & INTEGRITY…VOTE FOR KEN THOMPSON, CITY COMMISSION AT LARGE ON MARCH 14TH.

For Thompson, the assets he wanted to protect were the natural elements that made Sarasota so inviting: "If we don't destroy them [our geographical assets], we're going to stay in good shape—sunshine, the quality of the water and air, the beaches. We've got to keep these things properly burnished in our showcase. We've always said, 'Don't send us your industries, send us your industrialists.'"

In a field of eleven candidates, the *Herald* endorsed Thompson and Jack Gurney, the youngest and the oldest, saying, "These two men would bring to the City Commission the stability of age and experience and the innovative exuberance of a younger generation. We recommend Ken Thompson and Jack Gurney to the voters of Sarasota."

The *Herald* touted Thompson as a walking encyclopedia of information about the city: "His knowledge of Sarasota and Sarasota government is unsurpassed. He is honest. He does not cut ethical corners."

He was also endorsed in a letter signed by David Cohen, former mayor; K. Henderson, manufacturer; Jack Betz, former mayor; Jack West, architect, W. Ludi, retailer; and George Higgins, who had brought him, so long ago, to the attention of the city commission.

Calling themselves Sarasotans for Sarasota—and Ken Thompson, these men who had worked closely with Thompson over the years listed his qualifications and past accomplishments and wrote that it was "Thompson who advocates responsible growth—the kind that pays for itself and contributes to the entire city."

Not Quite Time to Say Goodbye

Photo of Thompson, Barbara and Muffin in their front yard, 1995. *Hime Photography, courtesy Barbara Thompson.*

The *Pelican Press*, which endorsed Gurney, speculated that the top four contenders were Bill Kline, Gurney, Linda Rosenbluth and Gene Pillot, who was a well-known former superintendent of Sarasota County schools.

With so many candidates running, City Manager David Sollenberger kidded that for the next election, they would modify the process: "Next time, we will do it in reverse. Everybody who isn't going to run will come in and register."

In a position paper for *Pelican Press*, Thompson indicated that he would improve minority relations. Compared to other southern cities, he noted, "relations between the city and African-Americans have been good. There were no burnings when other cities were; there were no hostile marches as were in other cities."

Economic improvement could be fostered in the Newtown area, "to develop ways for personal income to increase; the size of the paycheck is the ticket to participation in the social scheme."

Reporting that Thompson began with strong support, the *Pelican Press* indicated that at seventy-eight years old, some voters might decide he was too old for the four-year term but allowed that "he may have started with enough friends and firm supporters to win the election."

For his part, Thompson thought that his age played a factor in his being asked to retire.

As the two campaigned, Gurney was befriended by Thompson and grew to know him well. He found him to be very warm and genuine, quiet and dignified—statesman-like. Gurney called him a patrician gentleman.

Gurney, a reporter and editor for the weekly *Sarasota Times*, had covered city hall and said he always enjoyed talking to Thompson when he was city manager; he found him to be quite intelligent. "He could talk about any subject."

Gurney recalled that as city manager, Thompson believed that there was enough local brainpower and expertise for the city to solve its own problems without the need to go out of the area for help. "He was very parochial," said Gurney.

During the city commission campaign, Thompson thought he offered the voters a "package" and was perplexed that the public might not accept it.

He said to the *Times*, "I'm puzzled today as to why the package that I offer is not continuing to be purchased." He listed his qualifications, which were many, and went on, "I hate to say it but I still think...there is discrimination against the aged. I think a lot of it is saying move aside and let someone else have a chance to earn that money and perform those services."

When the votes were tallied, Thompson placed a credible third, with 1,544 votes, topping El Shahawy, 466; Ralph Garrabrant, 111; Kline, 1,459; Pattie Lanier, 1,520; Bill Michel, 429; Linda Rosenbluth, 1,451; George Saah, 236; and Alfredo Moreno, 342. The two winners were Gurney, with 2,564 votes, and Pillot, with 3,022.

Gurney also thought that perhaps age did factor into the election, conjecturing that if Thompson were ten years younger, he probably would have won.

Not Quite Time to Say Goodbye

The Commissioners
of the City of Sarasota
Cordially Invite You to Attend
the Formal Dedication
of
KEN THOMPSON PARK
at City Island

Friday, December 1, 1989
at 4 p. m.

Invitation for the dedication of Ken Thompson Park on City Island in appreciation for thirty-eight years of service to the city of Sarasota, which he so loved. *Courtesy Barbara Thompson.*

On December 1, 1989, "in recognition of his dedicated service to the City of Sarasota as City Manager," Ken Thompson Park on City Island was dedicated in his honor, along with a bas-relief marker.

It was a proud day for a proud man, a fitting tribute to the "Architect of Sarasota."

9
GOODBYE

I guess my greatest accomplishment lies in administering the needs of a growing community.
—*Ken Thompson*

Ken Thompson's long, rich, productive life came to an end on October 6, 2001. He was ninety-one years old, and by all accounts, he was a brilliant, industrious, kind and thoughtful gentleman whose word was his bond and his handshake as strong as a legal document. He was also a loving husband, father and grandfather.

Otherwise healthy, he had gone into the hospital for an elective surgery in early September 2001. He was still sailing and riding bicycles with his son Ken, who had come to town for a visit.

Postsurgical complications caused a decline in health. He went back to the hospital for three weeks, concerned less about himself than he was about the turmoil he felt he was causing his family.

Ken remembered how unassuming and kind his father was during this period—managing to joke, as best he could, with the nurses; being deflated and sad when he realized that Ken had flown back to Sarasota; and being concerned about the effect his poor health was having on Barbara.

After three weeks, when it seemed certain that he would not recover, the family acquiesced to his desire to go back to the family home in Harbor Acres—always his island of tranquility, his house of mirth.

His family cared for him for three weeks more before he passed away, surrounded by loved ones.

He was survived by his devoted wife, Barbara; his sons, Charles and Kenneth; his daughter, Laura Thompson DeUnger; and six grandchildren, Amanda, Alexandra, Chloe, Lain, Caroline and Miles.

The *Sarasota Herald*, always his champion, covered in detail his service to Sarasota. An editorial recounting his long and fruitful service said, "In an era of fast paced unprecedented change, throughout the world and locally, Thompson's life and career were models of endurance and stability. He was a man of the American century, and he was a central character in the formative half-century that produced modern-day Sarasota."

The paper termed the changes in Sarasota during Thompson's tenure "stunning" and added, "He had an honorable career in public service and lived a life to match. For a long, long time."

After his retirement as city manager, Thompson called Sarasota the best little city in the world and wrote of his role in creating it: "My part—to carry out the will of others. And to that end I hope I have performed appropriately and this beautiful creation of metal and stone will long attest to a period in Sarasota's history of a wonderful city undergoing a wonderful growth."

On April 2, 2002, the Kenneth Thompson Memorial Reflecting Pool in the city hall lobby was dedicated in his honor. Local dignitaries gathered with longtime supporters and citizens of all walks of life. There was a champagne toast and the unveiling of a plaque.

On the evening program, the citizens of Sarasota were reminded: "The water you drink, the parks you use, the streets you drive, the bay water in which you swim and sail upon, all bear the subtle thumbprint of Ken Thompson. His relentless patience in pursuit of excellence created the fruitful and majestic city we call Sarasota. One man, indeed, can make a profound difference."

10
TRIBUTES

Look, I don't want it to appear that I think he's God, but I don't think there has ever been anyone who has worked with him who hasn't respected him.
—*Unnamed former associate*

Mayor John Fite Robertson: "I have finished my first term of the commission, and, as I leave it, I want to express to you my appreciation for the high plane upon which you have conducted the city's business."

Mayor A. Ray Howard: "His ability, integrity and initiative, have afforded us the greatest single factor in the successful operation of our city." (*Sarasota Herald*, December 14, 1957)

Senator Bob Johnson: "He built the thing from scratch. Sarasota went from a one-stop-light town to the city it is today." (*Sarasota Herald*, October 6, 2001)

Newspaper reporter Rick Barry: "In 35 years there has never been so much as a whisper about Thompson's integrity, not so much as a free lunch, it is said, or a cocktail. He declines even a city-provided car." (*Tampa Tribune*, November 2, 1985)

Bill Overton, former mayor: "He never flaps. He has self-confidence. He has survived many commissions. His attitude is I was here when they came and I'll be here when they're gone." (*Florida Accent*, May 13, 1973)

Ed Hoyt, former Sarasota County administrator and former assistant to Thompson: "His temperament showed itself most strongly in the two periods when there was considerable antipathy toward retaining him. His ability to maintain an even temperament was a significant factor in his ability to weather this antipathy." (*Florida Accent*, May 13, 1973)

John O. Binns, former mayor: "I know of no man who has been so dedicated, worked more diligently, or contributed more to our fine City than has Ken Thompson during his 15 years of service." (Letter, December 7, 1964)

Jack Betz, former mayor: "We went out and spent money to bring in tourists, and Thompson was 100 per cent for it because the Commission wanted it. But he did have a calming effect on people who just wanted to rush out and do things." (*Florida Accent*, May 13, 1973)

Waldo Proffitt: "His honesty sets the tone for the whole city administration, and is the bedrock sort of thing that in time comes to be unquestioned." (*Sarasota Herald-Tribune* column, date unknown)

Lou Ann Palmer, mayor: "Without doubt, you epitomize the very essence of the best of that which is government service, and on behalf of all the citizens of Sarasota, the City Commission expresses its most sincere thanks and appreciation." (Letter to Thompson, April 4, 1989)

Al Rogero, former highway commissioner: "I worked with a great number of City Managers and Officials during my six years tenure as Highway Commissioner of the State of Florida and I want to say to you that I enjoyed working with you as much or more than any other official that I ran in to during the six years. I also want to say that the City of Sarasota should be very proud of what you accomplished for them and what you got for them..." (Letter to Thompson, May 15, 1973)

Judge John Scheb, former city attorney: "Ken was a role model of excellence in local government administration. Those of us who intimately shared the experience of working closely with Ken have been enriched and stimulated to emulate his concepts of professionalism." (From a speech delivered January 31, 1987, in the Thompson papers)

Appendix

A LIST OF CHANGES DURING THOMPSON'S TENURE

Bay Front Drive
Bobby Jones Golf Course Club House
Centennial Park
Condominium Row on Gulfstream Avenue
City hall
Flourescent downtown lighting
Island Park and Marina
Lido Beach restoration
Minor-league training facility
Mobile Home Park Auditorium
Newtown Improvement Program
North and South Downtown Loop
North and South Trail increased to four lanes
Orange Avenue Bridge
Public Safety Building
Purchase of North Lido Beach
Reclaimed Wastewater (REUSE) System
Rezoning downtown
Second Ringling Causeway
South Lido Park established
St. Armands Circle beautification
Street and highway beautification
10 MGD Reverse Osmosis Water Treatment Plant
Van Wezel Performing Arts Hall

BIBLIOGRAPHY

Berkel, Elmer, former mayor/commissioner. Interview, July 30, 2012; August 2, 2012.

City of Sarasota. Minutes of Regular City Commission Meeting of September 16, 1985. Ken Thompson papers.

DeUnger, Alexandra. Correspondence.

DeUnger, Laura Thompson. Correspondence.

Ferrell, John A. "The Day They Tried to Fire Kenneth Thompson." Undated paper on file at the Sarasota County History Center.

Florida Accent of the Tampa Tribune

The Florida Municipal Record, December 1966.

Franklin, Bruce. Interview, August 14, 2012.

Graham, Judy. Interview, August 1, 2012.

Grismer, Karl. *The Story of Sarasota*. N.p.: M.E. Russell Publishing, 1946.

Bibliography

Gurney, Jack, former mayor/city commissioner. Interview, July 19, 2012; August 2, 2012.

Hoyt, Ed, former assistant to Thompson and former county administrator. Interview, March 16, 2006.

Isle of Pines Appeal. N.p.: A.E. Willis, proprietor and publisher, December 1923.

James, Ed, community activist and host of *Black Almanac*. Interview, August 8, 2012.

Kirschner, Kerry, former mayor/city commissioner and president, Argus Foundation. Interview, August 9, 10, 2012.

Lewis, Amanda DeUnger. Correspondence.

The News

Palmer, Lou Ann, former mayor/city commissioner. Interview, August 3, 2012.

Pelican Press

Porter, Ray. "Faces: Ken Thompson." *Sarasota*, March 1982.

Proffitt, Anne. Interview with Ken Thompson, May 5, 1992. Ken Thompson papers.

Proffitt, Waldo, former newspaper editor for the *Sarasota Herald-Tribune*. Numerous articles and editorials.

Robertson, John Fite, former mayor/commissioner. Letter to Thompson, December 17, 1951. Thompson's personal papers.

Robinson, Billy, former city clerk. Interview, August 16, 2012.

Roehr, Rita, former mayor/commissioner. Interview, August 3, 2012.

Sarasota Herald-Tribune

Bibliography

Sarasota Journal

Smally, Don. *Sarasota and Me: An Engineer's Life (and Love) Story*. Sarasota, FL: Spotlight Graphics, Inc., 2009.

Soto, Fred E., former mayor/commissioner. Interview, August 5, 2012.

St. Petersburg Times

Thompson, Barbara. Numerous personal interviews.

Thompson, Ken and Charles. Correspondence.

Thorpe, Paul. Interview August 5, 2012.

Toner, Jim. "The Charmed Life of Ken Thompson." *Florida Accent*, May 13, 1973.

Weekly Times

West, Jack. *The Lives of an Architect*. Sarasota, FL: Fauve Publishing, 1988.

Zimmerman, Stan, reporter and author. Correspondence, August 28, 2012.

INDEX

A

Acker, Virginia Leigh 25, 32, 36, 115
American Legion War Memorial
    40, 42
Arvida Corporation 55, 56, 65,
    66, 111
Atkins, Fredd 127, 128, 129

B

Baldwin, Marge 133
Berkel, Elmer 9, 11, 90, 105
    105, 106, 131, 149
Betz, Jack 85, 88, 92, 94, 97,
    138, 146
Bickel, Karl 59, 67
    36, 67, 91
Binns, John 72
Bird Key 55, 56, 65, 66
Bischoff, Carl H. 16
Bloomer, John W. 15, 47
Burns, Owens 14, 17, 32, 62, 66, 159

C

Chidsey Library 46, 68, 69
Cohen, David 88, 94, 97, 133, 138

D

DeUnger, Laura Thompson 9,
    121, 144
Drymon, Ben 30, 32, 37, 57

E

Early, Mayor John 40, 44
Edwards, A.B. 14, 32, 40, 46

F

Farrell, Ralph 72
Fenne, Leroy T. 35
Flory, Roger 14, 90
Franklin, Bruce 149
Freeman, Forrest 44

G

Graham, Jack 82
Gulfstream Avenue 108, 109, 147

INDEX

Gulf Stream Towers 82, 110
Gurney, Jack 9, 11, 67, 138
   67, 139, 140, 150

H

Harmon, Mac W. 35
Hayo, Herschel 71, 85, 89
Hereford, Carolyn 132
Higgins, George 44, 133, 138
Hiss, Philip 84
Hoersting, Frank 62, 71, 72
Hopkins, Ben H., Jr. 44, 46
Hopkins, Ben, III 30, 32, 37, 44,
   46, 52, 57, 72
Hover Arcade 13, 57, 86, 90
Howard, A. Ray 61, 72, 145
Hoyt, Ed 66, 130, 146
   66, 150

J

Jackson, Elizabeth 39, 111
James, Ed 9, 68, 106
Jenkins, George 130
Johnson, Bob 145

K

Ken Thompson Park 141
Kicklighter, John 72
Kirschner, Kerry 9, 67, 127, 128,
   129, 130, 150
Kiwanis Club 14, 32
Kline, William 127, 128, 129, 138,
   139, 140

L

Lido Casino 71, 85, 90, 91, 94, 159
Lindsay Newspapers 103
Lord, Joseph 14

M

Marable, Eddie 61, 71, 72
memorial oak trees 42
Montgomery, William 88
Morton, Ted 130

N

Newtown 62, 67, 68, 85, 127,
   140, 147

O

Overton, William 13, 104

P

Palmer, Lou Ann 9, 88, 127, 128,
   129, 131, 132, 146, 150
Peters, William Wesley 98, 102
Pickett, Charles H. 32, 46, 62
Plymouth Harbor 85, 107
Proffitt, Waldo 12, 103, 126, 133, 146
Publix 130

R

Renshaw, Claude 30
Ringling Bridge 59, 62, 113, 132
Ringling Causeway 57, 62, 65, 78,
   82, 147
Ringling, Charles 14, 98
Ringling, John 14, 55, 56, 62, 66,
   77, 91
Robertson, John Fite 29, 35, 37, 145
Robinson, Billy 111, 135
Roehr, Rita 9, 108, 110, 127, 128,
   129, 138, 150
Rogero, Al 56, 64, 146
Rose, Glenn 88, 89
Rudolph, Paul 54, 57, 84

S

Saprito, Tony 94, 105, 113
Sarasota School of Architecture 54, 82, 87, 91
Saxe, Albert Moore 91
Scheb, John 103, 133, 146
Seibert, Tim 82, 84, 94, 109
Simmons, E.E. "Gene" 81, 87
Skandia Group 109
Smally, Don 66, 95, 151
Smith, Frank Folsom 85, 107
Sollenberger, David 131, 132, 134, 139
Soto, Fred 9, 97, 106, 107, 108, 111, 112, 126, 151
Sperling, Ted 66, 111
Sunshine Law 106

T

Taylor, Richard 128
Thomas, Robert 67
Thomas, Todd 118
Thompson, Barbara 9, 68, 102, 134
Thompson, Charles 17, 21, 27
Thompson, Kathleen 17, 22, 27
Thorpe, Paul 9, 113, 151
Twitchell, Ralph 91

W

Waters, Gil 66, 88, 104, 133
West, Jack 17, 21, 22, 84, 87, 88, 92, 97, 100, 102, 110, 138, 151
Williams, Mel 59
Wilson, Robert 44
Windom, Dr. Robert 16
Windom, Ross 32
Works Progress Administration 13, 53, 90, 98

Z

Zimmerman, Ralph 46
Zimmerman, Stan 86
Zimmerman, William 46, 55, 57, 84, 85

ABOUT THE AUTHOR

Jeff LaHurd moved with his family to Sarasota in 1950. He attended school at St. Martha's and Cardinal Mooney and graduated from Sarasota High. He has a bachelor's degree in history and a master's degree in counseling from the University of South Florida. He has been researching and writing about Sarasota's history for over twenty years.

Jeff and his wife, Jennifer, have four children. He is employed as the history specialist for Sarasota County and is a regular contributor to the *Sarasota Herald-Tribune* and other local publications. His video, *Sarasota, Landmarks of the Past*, was shown on the History Channel and won the Award for Communication from the Florida Trust for Historic Preservation.

OTHER BOOKS BY THE AUTHOR

Come On Down: Pitching Paradise During the Roaring '20s
Gulf Coast Chronicles: Remembering Sarasota's Past
Hidden History of Sarasota
John Hamilton Gillespie: The Scot Who Saved Sarasota
The Lido Casino: Lost Treasure on the Beach
Owen Burns: The Man Who Bought and Built Sarasota
A Passion for Plants: Marie Selby Botanical Gardens
Quintessential Sarasota
Sarasota: A History
Sarasota: Roaring Through the Twenties
Sarasota: A Sentimental Journey
Sarasota: Then and Now
Sarasota in Vintage Images
Spring Training in Sarasota, 1924–1960

Visit us at
www.historypress.net